Statistical Cost Analysis

STATISTICAL COST ANALYSIS

J. Johnston

PROFESSOR OF ECONOMETRICS
THE UNIVERSITY OF MANCHESTER

McGRAW-HILL BOOK COMPANY, INC.

New York   Toronto   London   1960

STATISTICAL COST ANALYSIS

III

Editor's Introduction

For years many teachers of economics and other professional economists have felt the need of a series of books on economic subjects that is filled neither by the usual textbook nor by the highly technical treatise.

This present series, published under the general title of *Economics Handbook Series*, was planned with these needs in mind. Designed first of all for students, the volumes are useful in the ever-growing field of adult education and also are of interest to the informed general reader.

The volumes present a distillate of accepted theory and practice without the detailed approach of the technical treatise. Each volume is a unit, standing on its own.

The authors are scholars, each writing on an economic subject on which he is an authority. In this series the author's first task was not to make important contributions to knowledge—although many of them do—but so to present his subject matter that his work as a scholar will carry its maximum influence outside as well as inside the classroom. The time has come to redress the balance between the energies spent on the creation of new ideas and on their dissemination. Economic ideas are unproductive if they do not spread beyond the world of scholars. Popularizers without technical competence, unqualified textbook writers, and sometimes even charlatans control too large a part of the market for economic ideas.

In the classroom the *Economics Handbook Series* will serve, it is hoped, as brief surveys in one-semester courses, as supplementary reading in introductory courses, and in other courses in which the subject is related.

The editor is very glad to have this interesting and able book by Professor Johnston on *Statistical Cost Analysis*.

The purpose of this book is to provide an up-to-date and comprehensive survey of the field of statistical cost functions. This begins with the review of the various economic hypotheses about how costs of production vary with the rate of output and the scale of a firm's operations. It is shown how these hypotheses may be put in a form suitable for statistical testing. The problems of statistical estimation and testing in this field are then considered in the light of recent developments in the theory of econometrics, and an attempt is made to explain in a clear, nontechnical fashion the basic assumptions underlying the statistical techniques and the extent to which they are valid in this area of econometric research. A variety of statistical cost analyses is then presented in detail covering such industries as electricity generation, road passenger transport, food processing, insurance companies, building societies, and coal mining. These empirical studies are illustrated both numerically and graphically, and the exposition is such that a reader interested mainly in empirical results may study and understand these without worrying too much about the finer points of statistical and economic theory underlying the analysis. An account is also given of the main empirical work done by other authors in this field in the last 25 years and a concluding chapter presents a critical assessment of the present state of work in this field.

The book is not intended as a text; its purpose is to serve as a reference work for courses in economic theory, theory of the firm, business economics and business administration, operations research, and accounting.

The author has taught at the universities of Wales, Manchester, Harvard, and Wisconsin and is currently professor of econometrics at the University of Manchester, England.

Seymour E. Harris

Preface

One of the most important developments in economics in the last 25 years has been the increasing amount of statistical and econometric work. There has always been statistical work in the sense of collecting and tabulating data on economic subjects; the newer emphasis, however, is on the application of statistical techniques to the data in order to estimate economic relationships and to test various hypotheses about such relationships. We may hope to see in the future an ever-accumulating body of empirically tested propositions covering many fields of economic activity. There are, however, two major difficulties in the way.

First, an embarrassingly wide range of talents is required for successful work in the econometric field, involving as it does some mathematics, statistics, economic theory, a rare knowledge of statistical sources and data-handling techniques, and a feel for the institutional realities of the situation to which the data relate. We are stricken with the fear of being in the position of Professor Stigler's famous shoemaker, whose "single unit of learning ability is cultivated subject to diminishing returns." Econometric work, as it is usually written up, often requires an equally sophisticated audience.

Second, many economic relationships may possess only a somewhat transient validity, if they depend on changing institutional arrangements or evolving patterns of human behavior. Thus some part of each generation's econometric work may have to be done anew.

The present work presents an integrated survey of the field of statistical cost functions, including the mathematical formulation of the various hypotheses, the problems involved in the statistical analyses, and an assessment of the results of these analyses. Statistical cost analysis has interest and relevance for economists interested in the theory of the firm and also for students of business economics, operations research, and management science, since a knowledge of the basic cost conditions underlying the operations of the firm is a necessary prerequisite both for building a microeconomic theory of price and output behavior and also for many specific designs of optimal operating policies. The basic approach is to take accounting data on costs, output, and other relevant aspects of a firm's operations and by statistical analysis study the nature of the cost-output relationships. An attempt has been made throughout to keep the use of mathematical and statistical jargon to an essential minimum and to explain as simply as possible the meaning and results of each step in the analysis.

I am greatly indebted to the University of Wisconsin for a most stimulating and delightful sojourn with a minimal teaching load during the 1958–1959 academic year, when the final version of this manuscript was completed. An earlier draft was accepted by the University of Wales as a thesis for the Ph.D. degree. Thanks are due to the trustees of the Houblon-Norman Fund for a research grant, which helped with the expenses of collecting data. I am also grateful to the publishers of *The Oxford Economic Papers*, *The Manchester School of Economic and Social Studies*, *The Bulletin of the Oxford University Institute of Statistics*, *The Journal of Industrial Economics*, and *The Review of Economics and Statistics* for permission to use substantial portions of previous articles of mine. Finally a special vote of thanks goes to Anna Campbell for her efficient and painstaking help in preparing this manuscript for the press.

J. Johnston

Contents

ix

For
A., R., and M.

1

Introduction

The purpose of this study is to subject certain economic hypotheses about cost-output relationships to empirical testing. These hypotheses are concerned with the variation of production costs within a firm as the level of output changes, and economists have customarily concentrated their attention upon two major types of cost-output variation, the one being the "short period" variation, in which the firm's actions are subject to the constraint that certain factors of production (for example, plant, equipment, and buildings) cannot be quickly changed in amount, and the other being the "long period" variation, when no such constraint is operative. Starting from plausible-seeming hypotheses about the nature of the productive process, economic theorists have derived an elaborate family of cost-output relationships. These relationships have in turn served as a basic building block in the conventional theory of price formation and resource allocation, which was elaborated in the twenties and thirties and consolidated into all the best textbooks in the forties and fifties. It is important, from a practical point of view as well as from that of economics, that these hypotheses should be tested against all available and relevant empirical evidence. The main hypotheses about cost-output variation to be found in the literature are reviewed in detail in Chap. 2.

The statistical testing of economic hypotheses is a complex and hazardous operation. Scientifically designed experiments, such as those which may be conducted in studying chemical reactions or agricultural field trials, are impossible. Instead, the economic system grinds out its complex convolutions; the myriads of actors—consumers, firms, regulatory agencies, and governmental units—act and interact; a more or less imperfect collection of statistical agencies records, with varying degrees of error and omissions, partial, quantitative measures of this evolutionary economic process; and the poor econometrician comes along in the wake of the monster, gathering what data he can in an attempt to "test" various hypotheses about aspects of economic activity. In the field of cost analysis the first major difficulty is the extreme paucity of published data on costs and output, a difficulty that is aggravated by the secrecy that often surrounds unpublished data on these variables. Any extensive empirical work in this field generally involves the collection of suitable data as the first step. The second difficulty, which is especially troublesome in cost analysis, though it is present in most econometric investigations, is the adjustment of the data to put them in a form relevant to the theories under investigation. The third major problem is the validity of the statistical techniques and tests employed. Theoretical statistics has developed at an extremely rapid pace in this century, largely stimulated by problems in the natural sciences, and the assumptions underlying the derivation of statistical methods have often been chosen on grounds of mathematical convenience or relevance to some experimental problem. The econometrician who wishes to apply such methods to data consisting of observations on the behavior of a complex economic system must examine to what extent the economic model, which is assumed to have generated the empirical observations, is or is not in conflict with the assumptions underlying the statistical methods. Some assumptions, fortunately, are less important than others in the sense that their nonfulfillment does not completely invalidate the applications of the statistical technique. The problems of data correction and statistical methodology in cost-output analysis are discussed in Chap. 3.

Chapter 4 contains empirical studies of six selected industries for which the author was able to obtain the necessary data, either from published sources or by private extraction from accounting records. For coal mining, road passenger transport, and food processing the data were collected at first hand, whereas in the cases of electricity, insurance companies, and building societies the analysis is based on published figures. It is unfortunate, though perhaps inevitable, that no comprehensive information on production costs is obtained in the census of production inquiries either in the United Kingdom or the United States. These inquiries do, however, give valuable information on important components of cost, such as those relating to labor and raw materials, but the confidential nature of this information renders grouping necessary before publication. It has been shown that apparently very different cost-size relationships emerge from a *given set* of census data according to the choice of size variable by which firms are grouped. Section 4-7 presents a full analysis of this problem together with suggestions on the interpretation of census data.

The two concluding chapters are designed to survey the field of statistical cost analysis. Chapter 5 contains a summary of the results of many important statistical cost studies made in the last 20 to 30 years, along with brief comments on the merits and deficiencies of the pieces. A considerable body of criticism of these statistical results has developed. The major criticisms are reviewed in Chap. 6, and the book concludes with an assessment of the impact of this work on the theory of the firm, along with some suggestions for future research.

2

Theoretical Hypotheses about the Relationships between Costs and Output

A firm utilizes a variety of productive services per unit of time to produce a certain flow of output. The relationship between costs and output then depends essentially upon two things: (1) the production function and (2) the conditions of supply of the factors of production to the firm.

In a firm producing a single homogeneous product the production function can be stated simply as the relationship describing the maximum flow of output per unit of time achievable for any given rates of flow of input services per unit of time. We may write

$$x = f(w,y,z, \ldots) \qquad (2\text{-}1)$$

where x denotes the rate of output and w, y, z denote rates of input per unit of time, all measured in physical terms. The first important assumption made about Eq. (2-1) is that it is a single-valued function; that is, for any given collection of w, y, z values, (2-1) specifies one and only one value of output x, and that value is the maximum rate of output technologically feasible with the specified rates of factor inputs.

The second important assumption relates to the *possibilities* of joint variation of the output x with the input services w, y, z. For some at least of the input services continuous variation over specified nonnegative values is assumed to be possible, and x is a continuous function with continuous partial derivatives of the first

4

and second order with respect to these services. Put differently, this assumption states that it is possible to vary some of the inputs, singly or in combination, by small amounts from any initial position, and the resultant output will change smoothly and will not be subject to sharp jumps. This emphasizes the possibility of continuous substitution of one input service for another input, again without causing sharp jumps in output. A production function that would *not* satisfy this assumption would be one where factors A and B had to be in exactly the right proportions, say 2 to 1, for any output to be possible. Then all input combinations such as $(2A, 0B)$, $(2A, 0.8B)$, $(2A, 0.9B)$, $(2A, 0.95B)$, $(2A, 0.99B)$ would yield zero output, while $(2A, 1B)$ would yield, say, one unit of output.

The third important assumption about the production function (2-1) relates to the *nature* of the joint variation of the output x and the input services w, y, z, etc. It is traditional to consider this in two stages: In the first, the analysis is confined within some assumed unit time period which is such that not all service inputs can be varied (the "short" period); cost curves are then constructed which picture the best results that the firm can achieve within the time constraint assumed. In the second stage, no time constraint is imposed at all (the "long" period), and the analysis is concerned with how costs vary in relation to output, when all inputs may conceivably be adjusted to achieve the optimal combination for each hypothetical output level. Those factors of production, whose rate of input may be varied in the short period, are defined as *variable* factors, and it is customary to classify factors into variable and fixed and to classify categories of cost in the same way.

We notice first of all that the distinction between fixed and variable is a relative one, depending upon the unit period of time to which the analysis refers. Secondly, factors may be classified as fixed or variable either on the basis of how their total cost behaves or on how their rates of input (services) can be changed, and the two classifications are by no means identical. For example, a firm may hire a number of machines at a fixed annual rent: the number of machines used and the hours of operation per machine may both be capable of variation, so that the rate of input of machine services is variable while their total cost is fixed. Or a firm may borrow funds at a certain rate of interest in order to purchase machinery, which then depreciates year by year through obsolescence and wear and tear. The annual machine costs may then split into the two categories of fixed and variable, with interest charges and depreciation due to obsolescence in the former category and wear and tear depreciation in the latter, while, if the assumptions of the previous example hold, the whole of the machine services is a variable input.

A classification of factors is also made sometimes on the basis of whether or not they are durable, but again this dichotomy need not coincide with either of those distinguished above. A durable factor may be defined as one which yields productive services over several periods of time, and the nondurable is one whose services are fully used up within the period of time under consideration; the distinction is once again seen to be relative to the unit time period assumed in the analysis. It is clear that a durable factor like machinery need not necessarily give rise to a fixed rate of machine services nor even to a fixed rate of cost per unit of time. So far as the firm's cost curves are concerned, the first two classifications are relevant, that is, whether for a given factor the total cost per unit of time is fixed or variable and whether the rate of input per unit of time is fixed or variable. Some possible situations for any single factor are shown in the accompanying table. This

Total cost *per unit of time*	*Rate of input* *per unit of time*
Wholly fixed	{ Fixed { Variable
Part fixed, part variable	Variable
Wholly variable	Variable

classification is not exhaustive, for it excludes cases where the cost of a factor may be wholly or partly variable, while its rate of input is fixed. Such cases, although logically possible, are difficult to illustrate with real life examples.

With respect to the nature of the joint variation of output and inputs, the ideal situation is described by Stigler[1] as follows:

> Production functions are descriptive of techniques or systems of organization of productive services, and they are therefore taken from disciplines such as engineering and industrial chemistry: to the economic theorist they are the data of analysis.

[1] G. J. Stigler, *The Theory of Price*, The Macmillan Company, New York, 1947, p. 109.

I say "ideal" situation because this account does not describe reality; it gives the unfortunate impression that there exists a large body of varied information which is both well authenticated and readily available to economists and the consultation of which has led them to frame generalizations, such as the law of variable proportions, which are descriptive of a variety of agricultural, industrial, and commercial situations. In fact, extensive data of the kind referred to exist mainly and almost wholly for agriculture.[1] However, hypotheses need not be founded on empirical data, and economists have not hesitated to postulate the existence of a production function with certain properties.

Two typical examples of the most common generalization about the joint variation of output and inputs in the short period are given below:[2,3]

> If the quantity of one productive service is increased by equal increments, the quantities of the other productive services remaining fixed, the resulting increments of product will decrease after a certain point. . . . The units of the variable productive service are homogeneous. The presence of diminishing returns is not due to the employment of less and less efficient men, for example, but because men of equal ability are being employed less efficiently.

> When the proportion of agencies in a combination is continuously varied over a very wide range, there is generally a first stage in which the product per unit of either agency increases; then a stage in which the product per unit of the relatively increased agency decreases and the product per unit of the relatively decreased agency increases, and finally a third stage in which the product relative to either agency decreases.

Each statement has at times been identified as the law of variable proportions, though there is an essential difference between them in that the first refers to diminishing marginal product and the second to diminishing average product, and indeed the one need not involve the other.

[1] See, for example, the only two references cited by Stigler: F. L. Patton, *Diminishing Returns in Agriculture*, Columbia University Press, New York, 1926, and W. J. Spillman and E. Lang, *The Law of Diminishing Returns*, World Book Company, Yonkers, N.Y., 1924.

[2] Stigler, *op. cit.*, pp. 116–117.

[3] F. H. Knight, *Risk, Uncertainty and Profit, Reprints of Scarce Works on Political Economy*, London School of Economics Series, no. 16, 1933, p. 99.

In the absence of any extensive empirical basis for the proposition of diminishing marginal product, attempts have been made to "prove" it, using a *reductio ad absurdum* method of proof. This type of proof was originally examined by Menger in two articles in *Zeitschrift für Nationalökonomie* in 1936, but these failed to gain the attention they merited in the English-speaking world, and the two papers have recently been combined into one by the author and published in an English translation.[1]

Menger shows first of all that the two propositions of diminishing marginal product (*diminishing product increment*) and diminishing average product do not necessarily involve one another. This he does by stating two production functions, one of which satisfies the property of diminishing product increments but not that of diminishing average product, and the other of which satisfies the property of diminishing average product, but not that of diminishing marginal product.[2]

The first type of "proof" of the law of diminishing product increments was based essentially on the assumption that the production function was bounded, that is, that output could not be increased indefinitely by additional outlay upon any one factor alone, but Menger shows, by an example due to F. Alt, that "neither diminishing product increments nor diminishing average products are a necessary consequence of the boundedness of the production function."[3] All that follows strictly from the assumptions that the production function is (*a*) bounded and (*b*) nondecreasing is an assertion intersecting the proposition of diminishing product increments. Letting $E(x,y)$ denote the output obtained from x units of, say, land and y units of a cooperating factor, then the intersecting assertion[4] is "For every x, for every y, and for every h for which

$$E(x, y_1 + h) \neq E(x,y_1), \text{ there exists a } \bar{y} = \psi(x,y_1,h) > y_1,$$

such that for every $y_2 > \bar{y}$

$$E(x, y_2 + h) - E(x,y_2) < E(x, y_1 + h) - E(x,y_1)."$$

[1] See Karl Menger, "The Laws of Return: A Study in Meta-economics," in Oskar Morgenstern (ed.), *Economic Activity Analysis,* John Wiley & Sons, Inc., New York, 1954, part III.

[2] *Ibid.* See fig. 1 on p. 427 and the two production functions given there.

[3] *Ibid.*, p. 446.

[4] *Ibid.*, p. 448.

Menger summarizes the difference as follows:[1]

Of the proposition of diminishing product increments and the intersecting assertion, the latter is stronger insofar as it compares product increments even in cases where one of the two outlays which are to be increased is not large: the former is stronger insofar as (where both outlays in question exceed a certain magnitude) it compares the product increment due to the addition to the smaller outlay with the increment due to the same addition to any larger outlay and not only to any larger outlay which is sufficiently large.

In the second type of classical proof due to Böehm-Bawerk and Wicksell, $E(x,y)$ is *assumed* to be

1. Subhomogeneous: that is, if land and the other factor are increased in the same proportion, the product increases at most in the same proportion
2. Increasing with respect to x: that is, with y units of the cooperating factor, if $x' < x''$, $E(x',y) < E(x'',y)$

But, as Menger shows, what follows from these two assumptions is not the law of diminishing product increments, but rather the law of diminishing average product, and as has been shown the existence of the latter does not necessarily imply the existence of the former. Finally, to round off a formidable article, Menger shows that even if to the above two assumptions we add any selection from the following three further assumptions, namely,

1. That land and the other factor are *either* independent factors (in the sense that each could produce some output with zero supply of the other) *or* dependent factors
2. That the production function is bounded with respect to both land and the other factor
3. That the product of an outlay on factors cannot be increased by division of that outlay into two separate parts

it is still not possible to "prove" the law of diminishing product increments, in the sense of showing that it is a necessary logical consequence of the assumptions made.[2]

The net result of Menger's work is to demote the law of diminishing product increments from the position of being necessarily true and to place it alongside other promising hypotheses for empirical testing.

[1] *Ibid.*, p. 449.
[2] *Ibid.*, pp. 465–470.

If, for the sake of simplicity, we assume that the production function contains only two inputs, one fixed and one variable, and if we also make the joint assumption of diminishing marginal and diminishing average product after some point for the variable factor, and if we finally assume a constant price for the variable

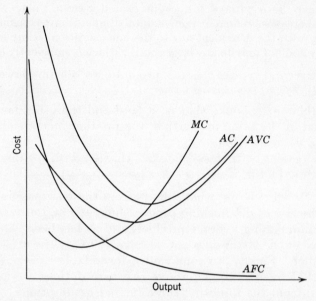

Fig. 2-1

factor, it is easy to illustrate the relationship between the production function and the short-run cost function. Defining the following symbols:

$$a = \text{number of units of variable factor}$$
$$p = \text{price per unit of variable factor}$$
$$MP = \text{marginal productivity of the variable factor}$$
$$AP = \text{average productivity of the variable factor}$$
$$x = \text{number of units of output}$$
$$AVC = \text{average variable cost per unit of output}$$
$$MC = \text{marginal cost}$$

we then have

$$AVC = \frac{pa}{x} = \frac{p}{AP}$$

$$MC = \frac{d(pa)}{dx} = \frac{p}{MP}$$

Thus these basic cost components are *inversely* related to the marginal and average products of the variable factor. If we assume the latter to rise smoothly at first and then fall, the cost curves behave in the opposite fashion and so we have the traditional U-shaped cost curves, enshrined in the textbooks and pictured in Fig. 2-1.[1]

The removal of the assumption of constant factor prices would not materially alter the shape of the curves in Fig. 2-1; the only difference would be to make the rise in MC, AVC, and AC earlier and greater.

In the above traditional treatment, there is assumed to be only a single variable factor and the output is taken to be a single homogeneous product. An attempt to widen these assumptions was made by Carlson and by Hicks.[2] But the assumption of diminishing product increments is carried over to the more general case, as Hicks goes on to state[3]

> If each factor out of a particular group is increased by an arbitrary increment, and a set of product-increments is found, whose production is made possible by the increase in the factors; if then a second equal increment is added to each of the factors, this second set of factor increments will not suffice to produce a second set of product-increments equal to the first.

> One consequence of this last rule is that the marginal cost (in money terms) of producing a particular product must rise when output increases, even if the supplies of all factors (except the fixed productive opportunity) are treated as variable.[4]

The important assumptions made in this multiproduct, multifactor case are that both product and factor proportions can be changed at will, subject only to the famous stability conditions of diminishing marginal rate of transformation of factor into product, increasing marginal rate of substitution of one product for another, and diminishing marginal rate of substitution of one

---

[1] A complete derivation of the steps from production function to cost function for the case of more than one variable factor is given in the Appendix to this chapter.

[2] Sune Carlson, *A Study on the Pure Theory of Production*, Stockholm Economic Studies, no. 9, P. S. King & Staples, Ltd., London, 1939; J. R. Hicks, *Value and Capital*, 1st. ed., Oxford University Press, New York, 1939.

[3] Hicks, *op. cit.*, footnote 2, p. 87.

[4] *Ibid.*, p. 87.

factor for another. But it is important to notice that these are the conditions required for stability if the firm is operating in perfectly competitive product and factor markets.

A second hypothesis about the nature of cost-output variation

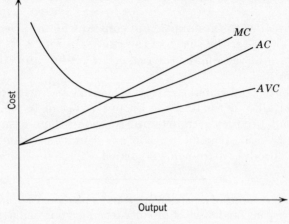

Fɪɢ. 2-2

is provided by H. T. Davis.[1] Denoting output by u and total costs by $Q(u)$, he writes:

$$Q(u) = au^2 + bu + c \qquad (2\text{-}2)$$

so that average cost has the form

$$q(u) = au + b + \frac{c}{u} \qquad (2\text{-}3)$$

and we thus have the curves pictured in Fig. 2-2. Davis states: "Such data as exist on cost functions show that (2-2) and (2-3) are essentially correct representations of total and average cost functions" yet later in the same chapter, in answer to the question, "What does a cost curve actually look like?" he quotes Yntema's study of the United States Steel Corporation[2] which gave

$$Q(u) = 182.1 + 55.73u$$

[1] H. T. Davis, *The Theory of Econometrics*, Principia Press, Bloomington, Ind., 1941, p. 125.

[2] T. O. Yntema, *Steel Prices, Volume, and Costs*, United States Steel Corporation, Temporary National Economic Committee Papers, vol. I., 1940, pp. 223–323.

where $Q(u)$ is measured in millions of dollars and u in millions of tons.

This total cost function for the United States Steel Corporation is an illustration of the third main hypothesis about the short-period variation of costs with output. This has been expounded mainly in the writings of P. W. S. Andrews.[1] His conclusion from an analysis of the short-period situation is

> In general, average direct costs per unit of product will be expected to remain constant over large ranges of output, so long as the business continues to employ the same methods of production, and the total of such costs will vary proportionately with total output.

This hypothesis leads to the situation depicted in Fig. 2-3. We thus have three distinct hypotheses about the nature of cost-output variation in the short period, of which the first commands fairly widespread support. The second, advanced by Davis without any empirical evidence or supporting rationalization, does not differ essentially from the first, and like it gives rise to a U-shaped average cost curve. The third is the most recent hypothesis and is

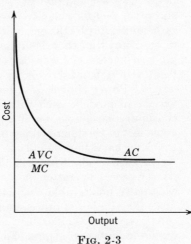

FIG. 2-3

the one suggested as most plausible by the accumulating empirical evidence.

Somewhat at a tangent to this discussion of cost curves, there has been a rapid development in recent years of the theory and practical applications of linear programming. One impact of this development on the theory of the firm has been the suggestion of a radically different set of assumptions about the nature of the productive activities of a firm, and the consequences of these assumptions for the firm's cost curves have not yet been fully worked out.

As is evidenced by Hicks's treatment of the production function,

[1] P. W. S. Andrews, *Manufacturing Business*, The Macmillan Company, New York, 1949, p. 102.

the traditional assumptions have involved the possibility of continuous substitution between factors or products and continuous transformation of factors into products (continuous in the mathematical, not temporal, sense), the rates of substitution and transformation being appropriately increasing or decreasing as the case may be. To this the linear programmers reply:[1]

> This model of production . . . very likely is valid for some kinds of production. But for most manufacturing industries, and indeed all production where elaborate machinery is used, it is open to serious objection. It is characteristic of most modern machinery that each kind of machine operates efficiently only over a narrow range of speeds and that the quantities of labour, power, materials and other factors which co-operate with the machine are dictated rather inflexibly by the machine's built-in characteristics. Furthermore, at any time there is available only a small number of different kinds of machinery for accomplishing a given task . . . . Earth may be moved by hand shovels, by steam or diesel shovels, or by bulldozers. Power shovels and bulldozers are built in only a small variety of models, each with inherent characteristics as to fuel consumption per hour, number of operators and assistants required, cubic feet of earth moved per hour, etc. Printing type may be set by using hand-fonts, linotype machines or monotype machines. Again, each machine is available in only a few models and each has its own pace of operation, power and space requirements, and other essentially unalterable characteristics . . . . For many economic tasks the number of processes available is finite, and each process can be regarded as inflexible with regard to the ratios among factor inputs and process outputs. Factors cannot be substituted for each other except by changing the levels at which entire technical processes are used, because each process uses factors in fixed characteristic ratios. In mathematical programming, accordingly, process substitution plays a role analogous to that of factor substitution in conventional analysis.

A productive process can thus be completely specified by the vector stating the quantities of the factors required to operate the process at unit level (where the unit level may be defined in any way convenient, as, for example, the level of the process at which one unit of product is produced). The function is taken to be homogeneous of the first degree, a doubling of output requiring a doubling of all inputs.

[1] R. Dorfman, "Mathematical or 'Linear' Programming," *American Economic Review*, vol. 43, no. 5, December 1953, p. 803.

The linear programming theory is essentially a short-run theory, and a distinction is therefore made between fixed and variable factors.[1]

> The entrepreneur already has under his control a complex of goods, the equipment of the firm. Equipment includes, land, buildings, machinery, tools, raw materials, goods in process, goods technically finished but not yet sold. Now it does seem reasonable to assume that this equipment will have acquired some organic unity, so that it cannot be exactly reduplicated at a moment's notice. It is the firm's legacy from the past and, as such, does seem to constitute a block of "fixed resources" in the relevant sense.

Dorfman[2] suggests the addition to this list of the permanent and integrated staff of the establishment, and he concludes: "Within a short time period these resources limit absolutely the opportunities available to the firm, and in a dynamic context they limit the firm's rate of growth."

For a firm in a perfectly competitive position the variable factors are assumed to be freely available in unlimited quantities at the ruling market prices.[3] Consequently their contribution to unit costs in a given process is *constant*, whatever the level of the process. To study the firm's decisions, therefore, the vectors specifying the productive processes need only state the amounts of the fixed factors required. Assuming only two fixed factors, productive processes may be shown as in Fig. 2-4. The point L on the ray OA represents the unit level (one unit of product) of process A, and it is seen that this requires amount a_1 of the first scarce factor and a_2 of the second. The productive processes may thus be specified by the vectors $P_A = \begin{pmatrix} a_1 \\ a_2 \end{pmatrix} P_B = \begin{pmatrix} b_1 \\ b_2 \end{pmatrix}$ and $P_C = \begin{pmatrix} c_1 \\ c_2 \end{pmatrix}$. It is

---

[1] Hicks, *op. cit.*, pp. 199–200.

[2] R. Dorfman, *Application of Linear Programming to the Theory of the Firm*, University of California Press, Berkeley, Calif., 1951, p. 86.

[3] A variable factor is not quite the same thing in the linear programming as in the traditional analysis. In both analyses it is a factor whose amount can be freely varied in the short run, but in the linear programming analysis increases in the variable factors, unaccompanied by any increase in the amounts of the fixed factors used, will yield no additional output. It is clear also that "fixed" in the linear programming analysis refers only to the existence of an upper limit on the amount available for use: it is explicitly assumed in the analysis that the amount actually used per unit of time can be freely varied up to that limit.

further assumed in the linear programming theory that the processes are *independent* and *additive*, that is, that operating process A at level λ requires λa_1 units of the first factor and λa_2 of the second, and yields λ units of output, irrespective of the levels at which B and C are operated, and further that the operation of the three processes at levels λ_A, λ_B, and λ_C, respectively, yields $(\lambda_A + \lambda_B + \lambda_C)$ units of output and requires $(\lambda_A a_1 + \lambda_B b_1 + \lambda_C c_1)$ units

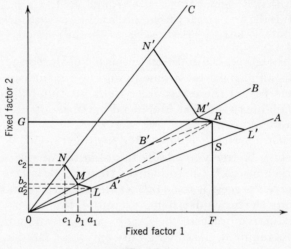

Fig. 2-4

of the first factor and $(\lambda_A a_2 + \lambda_B b_2 + \lambda_C c_2)$ units of the second. Any point lying between two process rays represents a production program in which two processes are operated in the same time period at nonzero levels; for example, point R on the line segment $M'L'$ represents the operation of process A at level OA' and process B at level OB', $B'R$ being parallel to OA and $A'R$ parallel to OB. The total consumption of the first fixed factor under this program is OF and of the second OG. If we join the points N, M, L representing the unit levels of the three processes and then through R draw $M'L'$ parallel to ML and also draw $N'M'$ parallel to NM, the broken-line segment $N'M'L'$ is an isoquant showing all production programs which give the same output as, for example, that achieved by operating process A alone at level OL'.

Suppose that in fact OF and OG represent the total amounts available of the two fixed factors. Then all points in the rectangle

OFRG represent feasible production programs with the maximum possible output being achieved at point *R*, which lies on the highest isoquant.

Our immediate concern is with the behavior of production costs as output is varied over the range from zero to the limit represented by *R*. There are very many paths by which output might be expanded from zero up to the maximum possible; for example, we might first of all use process *A* only, until we encounter at *S* the barrier set by the limited amount of the first fixed factor. Output can still be expanded, however, beyond the level represented by *S* by considering production programs represented by points on the line *SR*. Advancing from *S* to *R* implies an ever-diminishing level of operation for process *A* and an increasing level of operation of process *B*, until at *R* the former operates at level *OA'* and the latter at level *OB'*. Similarly we might commence by using process *C* only, then a combination of *C* and *B* with ever-diminishing emphasis on the former until it is eventually replaced by *A* and the point *R* is reached once again.

We cannot tell from Fig. 2-4 which of these output paths will be adopted. The choice depends on (1) the nature of the costs of the two fixed factors and (2) the cost of the variable factors per unit of output in each of the processes.

To illustrate the nature of the cost curves, we shall take a numerical example. Suppose that we have just two processes *A* and *B* with two fixed factors and that the process vectors are $P_A = \begin{pmatrix} 1 \\ 0.5 \end{pmatrix}$ and $P_B = \begin{pmatrix} 0.5 \\ 1 \end{pmatrix}$. Suppose further that the costs of the two fixed factors are fixed per unit of time and that the average direct costs per unit of output are 75 cents for process *A* and 50 cents for process *B*. Those are the costs of the variable factors and will remain constant in each process per unit of output. Finally we assume that the total supply of the first fixed factor is 10 units and of the second 5 units.

Since process *B* has the lower direct costs, it will be used for all output levels up to and including 5 units of product; any attempt to obtain more than 5 units of product from process *B* would encounter the barrier of only 5 units of the second fixed factor being available. For these first 5 units of output, average direct cost and marginal cost are both constant at 50 cents. In order to produce 6 units of output without violating the restrictions on either fixed factor, the level of process *B* has to be reduced by 1 thus releasing 1 unit of the second fixed factor, which, in cooperation with 2 units of the first fixed factor, which is still in sufficient supply, can yield 2 units of output from process A. At this stage total utilization of the two fixed factors is given by

$$2\binom{1}{0.5} + 4\binom{0.5}{1} = \binom{4}{5}$$

Total variable cost is \$3.50, so that marginal cost is \$1 and average variable cost is \$0.583. Proceeding in this way we obtain the figures given in Table 2-1.

TABLE 2-1
EXAMPLE OF COSTS OF PRODUCTION UNDER LINEAR
PROGRAMMING ASSUMPTIONS

Units of output (1)	Total variable cost, dollars (2)	Average variable cost, dollars (3)	Marginal cost, dollars (4)
1	\$0.5	\$0.5	\$0.5
2	1.0	0.5	0.5
3	1.5	0.5	0.5
4	2.0	0.5	0.5
5	2.5	0.5	0.5
6	3.5	0.583	1.0
7	4.5	0.643	1.0
8	5.5	0.687	1.0
9	6.5	0.722	1.0
10	7.5	0.750	1.0

These cost conditions are pictured in Fig. 2-5. The average variable cost curve is constant at first and then slowly rises asymptotically toward a new level; the marginal cost curve consists of discontinuous horizontal straight line segments, each successive segment at a higher level than its predecessor; and the total cost function is a series of straight line segments convex downward.

A very important point to notice here is that the total cost function is linear over substantial ranges of output, and this linearity holds not only when a single process is being used at various levels but also when two processes are being used simultaneously at varying levels, as is the case here over the output range from 6 to 10 units. This is important because demand conditions may be such as to prevent empirical observations over more than a single linear segment of the total cost function being generated. For example, if the firm in our example were faced with a perfectly competitive market for its product with a selling price of $1, there would be no point in producing more than 5 units of product, for units 6 to 10 would neither add to nor subtract from total profit.

To make the analysis somewhat more general we must relax the assumption that the *costs* of the fixed factors are wholly fixed per unit of time. Some part of these costs may well vary with the amount of each fixed factor actually utilized in the production

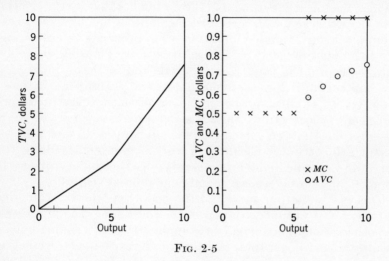

FIG. 2-5

program (wear and tear). If this element of cost were assumed to depend linearly on utilization, then the qualitative conclusion of the above analysis would be unchanged: the general shape of the cost functions would still be as pictured in Fig. 2-5, but the slopes of the total cost function would be steeper and *AVC* and *MC* correspondingly higher. If wear and tear were substantially greater for process *B* than for process *A* in the above example, it is possible that process *A* may become the process with the cheaper unit costs and the one used at the lower output rates, but it is clear that the general shape of the cost curves would be unaltered. If wear and tear were related in a nonlinear fashion to utilization, then some degree of curvilinearity would creep into each section of the total cost function.

The further generalization of the analysis to larger numbers of available processes and fixed factors would simply increase the number of segments in the total cost function and the number of horizontal steps in the marginal cost function, but these segments and steps would still be linear.[1]

There is one respect in which these linear programming assumptions seem almost as unsatisfactory as the assumptions underlying the traditional case of U-shaped cost curves outlined earlier. A difficult stumbling block in the latter was the manner in which a fixed supply of capital, say, was adapted or transformed so as to cooperate with different amounts of variable factors. In a similar fashion the linear programming theory implies that, as the level of one process is reduced, increased amounts of one or more fixed factors become available for use in other processes. Considering the fixed factors listed by Hicks,[2] it is fairly plausible to apply this assumption to land, raw materials and, perhaps, buildings, but implausible in the case of machinery and possibly also in tools. However, this difficulty is not really serious in the linear programming set of assumptions, since it is not a necessary part of those assumptions that *every* fixed factor should appear in each process vector; thus an over-all limit on machinery would be disaggregated into specific limits for several types of machinery, and each type might possibly appear in only one process vector.

This completes our survey of the main hypotheses about the nature of cost-output variation in the short run. The first three hypotheses may be conveniently summarized as yielding cubic, quadratic, and linear total cost functions, respectively, while the linear programming theory gives a total cost function consisting of linear segments.[3]

When the time constraint assumed in the foregoing analysis is removed, we consider how costs vary for different output levels when at each output level the most appropriate combination of all factors can be arranged. The common treatment of this case in the literature relies upon the laws of increasing and diminishing return. The former is assumed to operate almost universally in

---

[1] For a generalization to a multiproduct firm, see M. J. Beckmann, "Fixed Technological Coefficients and the Short Run Cost Curve," *Kyklos*, vol. 9, pp. 384–386, 1956.

[2] See p. 15 above.

[3] This is not meant to imply that cubic and quadratic functions are the only possible representations of the first two hypotheses. For example, $y = k_1 e^x + k_2 e^{-x}$ might well describe a U-type average cost curve. The polynomials are, however, very easy to fit and also lend themselves easily to statistical tests of the effect of including higher powers of the output variable.

the lower output ranges for a variety of reasons, about which there is fairly substantial agreement among various authors.[1]

Stigler,[2] in his *Production and Distribution Theories*, summarizes the major economies described by Marshall as

1. Economy of materials, or the utilization of by-products
2. Economy of machinery
   a. "In a large establishment there are often many expensive machines each made specially for one small use," which a small manufacturer cannot afford to use
   b. Larger machines are more efficient
   c. Small manufacturers are sometimes ignorant of the best types of machinery to use in their business
   d. Small manufacturers cannot undertake expensive experiments
3. Economy in the purchase and sale of materials
   a. Discount for quantity purchases—possibly lower freights
   b. Cheaper to sell in large quantities—better advertising coverage and fuller information regarding the market
4. Economy of skill
   a. Each man assigned to the task for which he is best fitted, where he acquires additional proficiency by repetition
5. Economy of finances

Sargant Florence approaches the problem in a slightly different way and sets out logical principles for "supposing economy and efficiency to result from large-scale production, carried on in one or (perhaps less forcibly) several organizations."[3] These principles are:

1. *Principle of Bulk Transactions.*[4] "Total monetary, physical, or psychological costs of dealing in large quantities are sometimes no greater (and in any case less than proportionately greater) than the costs of dealing in small quantities."

[1] See, for example, A. Marshall, *Principles of Economics*, 8th ed., The Macmillan Company, New York, 1938, chap. 9; E. A. G. Robinson, *The Structure of Competitive Industry*, rev. ed., Cambridge University Press, New York, 1935; A. Beacham, *Economics of Industrial Organization*, Sir Isaac Pitman & Sons, Ltd., London, 1948; and P. Sargant Florence, *The Logic of British and American Industry*, Routledge & Kegan Paul, Ltd., London, 1953.

[2] G. J. Stigler, *Production and Distribution Theories*, The Macmillan Company, New York, 1946, pp. 279–283.

[3] Florence, *op. cit.*, pp. 49–60.

[4] *Ibid.*, p. 50.

2. *Principle of Massed (or Pooled) Reserves.*[1] "Reserves that are economised may be labour, liquid monetary resources, stocks of goods and materials or any other factors in production, when the demands upon these factors are somewhat uncertain in their incidence."

3. *Principle of Multiples.*[2] Specialized men and machines must, for efficiency, be used in their speciality up to full capacity, but the capacities are different and indivisible. Thus we have the virtuous circle in which "specialization leads to higher common multiples, higher common multiples to greater specialization."

Florence more than most authors in this field deserves credit for distinguishing clearly between establishment (or plant) and firm, and for noting the factors which may be relevant to changes in scale of plant and/or firm. For the case of the large firm with a single plant and a single product, the major sources of economies[3] are

1. Increased specialization of labor
2. Increased use of specialized machinery
3. Lower administrative costs per unit of output

In the case of any large firm, whatever its substructure of plants and products, knowledge is available throughout the organization of patents, secret devices, and the results of technical and market research. Specific economies are[4]

1. Reduction of bad debts
2. Common use of patents, trade-marks, etc.
3. Power to command "big brains" and use their capacity to the full
4. Power to distribute subordinate management and skill among a variety of jobs according to capacity.

Finally, a large plant, whatever the firm substructure or product substructure, has specific economies available to it such as[5]

1. Reduction in the transport costs of moving output from process to process.
2. "Auxiliary services such as repairs and maintenance or tool-making, are more readily communicated with and brought to the

[1] *Ibid.*, p. 50.
[2] *Ibid.*, p. 52.
[3] *Ibid.*, p. 58.
[4] *Ibid.*, p. 60.
[5] *Ibid.*, p. 60.

spot if the services are part of the productive organization instead of being called in from outside."

3. "Communication of plans and orders more readily effected and their execution supervised within one plant than among several plants."

For all these reasons, there is fairly general agreement that average costs per unit of output are probably lower in the majority of trades the greater the scale of production of the plant or firm. It is likewise agreed that some finite level of production is usually sufficient to exhaust any given source of economy, so that beyond the scale of output needed to reconcile these varying optima costs will not decline any further. The one serious point of disagreement is on the behavior of costs when relatively large output levels are reached in particular firms. One school of writers holds that the power of the manager to coordinate and control is in effect an indivisible unit, or factor, which may be cultivated subject only to diminishing returns.[1]

> Despite the great advances made (in co-ordination and administration), however, there must come a point at which the machine is too unwieldy to be managed, a point at which the gains of increasing size are so negligible that the still increasing costs of co-ordination are likely to exceed them. In this the managerial optimum differs from the technical optimum. The latter affords only a minimum scale below which the greatest efficiency cannot be achieved. Additional output may be produced under conditions of approximately constant cost. But if the managerial optimum is exceeded, costs, through declining efficiency and the need for additional co-ordination, begin to rise. The managerial optimum sets, therefore, not only a lower but also an upper limit to the scale of operations.

Of the group of authors typified by the above quotation, Florence[2] says,

> In their opinion the management gets positively less efficient (not just no more efficient) after a certain size is passed, and they dogmatically (and often automatically) draw a curve of costs for the firm rising from left to right as the quantity of output increases. How many blackboards have been filled lecture hour by lecture hour in British and American universities with such exercises in draftsmanship. For it remains an exercise. There is little to prove the universality and inevitability of any such law of increasing

[1] Robinson, *op. cit.*, p. 48.
[2] Florence, *op. cit.*, p. 63.

costs in the long run when manufacturers have time to get new equipment in order to meet enlarged orders or anticipated orders and have time to reorganise and delegate responsibilities.

Business enterprise today is a corporate manifestation and its capacity to cope with large outputs is not fixed but expands with its structure—and depends on the relation between the governing members of the corporation.[1]

Most of those who have made a special study of organization differ from the economists. They come to the conclusion that no limit is set to the size of organization, if correct principles are adopted to enable a single leader to delegate control.[2]

Even if this last point of Florence's is correct, it does not disprove the economists' case which is, not that problems of coordination set a definite limit to the size of organization, but rather that these problems impose rising costs with scale.

The argument is by no means settled. After an initial and presumably often a substantial decline the long-run average cost curve may remain approximately constant, or it may rise. It remains to survey the available empirical evidence before reaching any final judgment.

Appendix: Mathematical Derivation of the Short-run Cost Function

The principles involved may be most simply demonstrated by assuming a specific type of production function. Let it be

$$x = kv_1^{\alpha}v_2^{\beta}v_3^{\gamma} \tag{A2-1}$$

where x denotes the rate of output, v_1, v_2, v_3 the rates of input of the variable factors, and k, α, β, and γ are parameters. Since we are interested in the short-run function we need not show the fixed factors explicitly but may let their influence be reflected by the multiplicative factor k. Total variable cost is

$$\Pi = \sum_{i=1}^{3} p_i v_i \tag{A2-2}$$

where p_i indicates the price per unit of the ith variable factor. The short-run problem is to maximize output for any given expenditure on variable factors. Defining

$$\phi = x - \lambda(\Sigma p_i v_i - \Pi)$$

[1] *Ibid.*, p. 64.

[2] *Ibid.*, p. 142.

where λ is a Lagrangian multiplier, and taking partial derivatives with respect to the v_i, and equating to zero gives

$$\frac{\partial x/\partial v_1}{p_1} = \frac{\partial x/\partial v_2}{p_2} = \frac{\partial x/\partial v_3}{p_3} \qquad \text{(A2-3)}$$

on the assumption that the factor prices are independent of the firm's purchases. This is the well-known result that the variable factors should be combined in such a way as to make their marginal physical productivities proportional to their prices. The same condition is also reached by solving the problem of minimizing total variable costs for any given output level.

Working out (A2-3) for the production function (A2-1) enables us to express v_2 and v_3 in terms of v_1

$$v_2 = \frac{\beta}{\alpha}\frac{p_1}{p_2}v_1 \qquad v_3 = \frac{\gamma}{\alpha}\frac{p_1}{p_3}v_1 \qquad \text{(A2-4)}$$

Substituting these back in the production function gives

$$x = k'v_1^{(\alpha+\beta+\gamma)} \qquad \text{(A2-5)}$$

where

$$k' = k\left(\frac{\beta p_1}{\alpha p_2}\right)^{\beta}\left(\frac{\gamma p_1}{\alpha p_3}\right)^{\gamma}$$

Taking the inverse of (A2-5) and substituting both (A2-4) and (A2-5) in (A2-2), we have

$$\Pi = k''x^{1/(\alpha+\beta+\gamma)} \qquad \text{(A2-6)}$$

where k'' is a constant depending upon the parameters of the production function and the prices of the variable factors. We see that if the exponents in this type of production function sum to unity, total variable cost will be linear, and average variable cost and marginal cost are both equal to the constant k''. If $(\alpha + \beta + \gamma) > 1$, average variable cost and marginal cost will both decline steadily with increases in output, while if $(\alpha + \beta + \gamma) < 1$ both will increase.

Removing the assumption of constant factor prices would change (A2-3) to

$$\frac{\partial x/\partial v_1}{\partial(p_1v_1)/\partial v_1} = \frac{\partial x/\partial v_2}{\partial(p_2v_2)/\partial v_2} = \frac{\partial x/\partial v_3}{\partial(p_3v_3)/\partial v_3}$$

which is that marginal physical productivities should be proportional to marginal factor costs. We could assume specific forms for the factor price functions $p_i = p_i(v_i)$ and then follow through the same steps as in (A2-3) to (A2-6) above.

3

Problems of Statistical
Estimation and Procedure

The problems of data gathering and rectification may best be introduced by considering what data we should ideally like in order to examine the validity of the various hypotheses outlined in Chap. 2. The hypotheses about short-run costs involve the assumption that the firm's activities are constrained by some fixed capacity limit. Thus we should ideally like a series of paired observations on costs and output which satisfied the following conditions.

1. The basic time period for each pair of observations should be one in which the observed output was achieved by a uniform rate of production *within* the period. It would not be desirable, for example, to have 4 weeks as the basic time period if there were substantial weekly variations in the rate of production, for the 4-week figures would then be averages which might obscure the true underlying cost curve.

2. The observations on cost and output should be properly paired in the sense that the cost figure is directly associated with the output figure. This condition would not be satisfied, for example, if we paired accounting data for weekly periods, where the wages paid in any given week were, in fact, based on the number of hours worked in the previous week.

3. We should also like a wide spread of output observations so that cost behavior could be observed at widely differing rates of

output. This result could be achieved by having a very large number of experimental firms, all of the same fixed capacity, and instructing each to produce at a certain rate, these arbitrary rates being chosen to give the desired range of output levels. Or we might have a small number of experimental firms, all of the same fixed capacity, and vary the rate of output over various periods of time. In both cases it would be necessary for the observations on any given rate of output to relate only to periods when the firm was fully adjusted to producing at that rate and doing so with maximum efficiency within the assumed capacity constraint.

4. It would also be necessary to keep the experimental data uncontaminated by the influence of factors extraneous to the cost-output relationship itself. For example, we should not wish to record cost observations which were influenced by variations in the prices paid by the firm(s) for factors of production such as labor, raw materials, etc. Secondly, we should not want different observations to relate to different environments of technical knowledge and expertise; instead, we should require that each firm in each period should have at its disposal the *same* stock of technical knowledge. We should not need to insist, in the short-run analysis, that the management of each firm be equally efficient in utilizing existing technical knowledge, since random variations in efficiency between firms of a given capacity can be handled in the statistical analysis. This factor, however, as we shall see below, would require a different treatment in the long-run analysis.

The four requirements above have been stated with reference to the ideal data for testing short-run cost-output relationships. To examine the long-run relationships, essentially similar requirements apply. The basic unit of time to which individual observations relate should again be short enough to avoid possible averaging effects, and the cost-output observations should again be properly paired. The requirement of a wide spread of output observations is more stringent than before, for we must now have observations on firms with widely different capacity limits, ideally ranging from very small to very large firms. This might be achieved by having a large number of experimental firms of widely differing sizes, and letting each produce at various rates within its capacity limit, or by having a smaller number of firms, which over various time periods assumed different sizes. In either case the statistical observations should only relate to periods when the firm is fully adjusted to both size and rate of output. Moreover it is still important that cost movements, due to factor price variations, should not appear in the data. The requirement about technical knowledge is now especially important. If small firms in an industry use different productive processes and factor proportions than large firms, this should not be the result, say, of smaller firms having been established at an earlier date with types of equipment and associated modes of production, which are not the most efficient, *for that scale of production*, in the light of current knowledge. We require, ideally, that each firm, of whatever scale, should be producing within that scale in the economically most efficient manner, given the current state of technology and the current range of factor prices. If, however, one consequence of the greater division of labor within larger firms is a greater exploitation and application of current technical knowledge through its planning and managerial personnel, then this factor is relevant to the inquiry and no attempt should be made to correct the statistical data for its influence. Thus in the long-run cost analysis this factor may not be randomly distributed with respect to size of firm. However, there is no very firm a priori expectation, since offsetting factors are the possibility of smaller firms using consulting services periodically to push themselves out toward the boundaries of their production functions and the possibly greater difficulties of coordination and control in the larger firms.

Given data satisfying the above requirements, it would be a relatively simple matter to examine the validity and practical relevance of various hypotheses about cost-output relationships. Real world firms, however, are not setting their output levels to achieve a statistically desirable spread of observations in a frictionless environment, free of extraneous and irrelevant variables. Rather, they are part of an evolutionary economic mechanism, and with imperfect foresight they chart a somewhat uncertain course in an attempt to satisfy as best they can certain continuing objectives of their own choosing. Thus, if we examined a large cross section of firms in a given industry, we should probably find very few with any given capacity limit. It would appear, therefore, that the best source of information for the short-run analysis would be the records of given firms over successive periods of time during which their capacity had remained unchanged. Granted that we can find a sufficient number of firms satisfying this capacity condition, there are still many difficulties. Published information, if it exists at all, may be for unit time periods which are undesirably long for purposes of a short-run analysis. Even with access to internal data, the researcher must usually content himself with working with the unit time period, which he finds in the firm's accounts. This accounting time period may still be a bad approximation to the unit time period relevant to the underlying economic theory. Some critics have alleged that the averaging, which is necessarily involved, will seriously bias the resulting statistical analyses, and we shall defer a thorough discussion of this point till Chap. 6. Successive output levels of a given firm may yield a very inadequate spread of observations, judged from the viewpoint of obtaining a good statistical determination of the cost-output relation. An attempt to widen the spread by continuing the observations over a greater number of time periods is likely to founder on a change in the firm's capacity, or, if not, various other changes may be at work. For example, improved productive practices may be spreading throughout the industry as time passes, the quality of the raw materials may be changing, the attitude of management to cost reduction may change with the phase of the business cycle, and so on. In general, changes which are random and unpredictable from period to period need not, and indeed cannot, be adjusted for and will show up in a greater "unexplained" or residual variation in the statistical analysis. The net effect of other changes that persist over time may be approximately isolated by the inclusion of time as an explanatory variable. This last procedure is not suitable if the direction of these trend effects changes during the time range observed or if the influences involved are so important and sufficient data exist to enable a more direct and flexible adjustment for their effect to be made. An example of this latter category is factor price changes. The usual procedure is to adjust the observed cost data for factor price changes period by period, and to employ only the adjusted data in the statistical analysis. The adjustment may be carried out by deflating total costs with some factor price index number or by recalculating costs each period by applying some chosen set of constant factor prices to the actual rates of factor input in each period. It has been suggested that these methods of data correction also impart substantial biases to the results of the statistical analyses, and this question is also taken up in Chap. 6.

The desired range of output observations in the long-run analysis can probably only be obtained from "cross-section" data for a reasonably large number of firms at some given period of time. This automatically rules out the possibility of temporal variations in factor prices distorting the cost-output relation, but it does admit the possibility of effects from spatial variation in factor prices. If these are systematically connected with size of firm, then they may or may not require correction. If, for example, the price of a certain raw material is low in a given area because the presence of a very large firm in that area is primarily responsible for large-scale production of the raw material at low unit cost, then a case could be made for leaving that price effect uncorrected as being a consequence of scale. In general, however, such clear-cut cases will be so rare that it is probably best to correct for spatial price variations if they are judged important relative to other factors and if data exist for such corrections. More substantial variations are probably due to the fact that cross-section data for a given year, say, will picture each firm at a different point on its evolutionary path. The various installations of fixed plant and equipment will reflect in crystallized fashion the technologies and ideas of various bygone ages, and may often be a poor approximation to the current long-run curve, which would picture the best results achievable at various scales of output, given the current state of technology. The cross-section approach will obviously work best in an industry subject to slow technical change. If technical change were uniformly rapid for all size groups and if age of equipment were randomly distributed with respect to size, various ages of plant and equipment in a cross-section survey would produce discrepancies about the true cost-scale line but would not essentially distort it. However, if the larger plants were, on the average, much newer than the old and if technical progress had not been concentrated at the upper end of the size scale, then the cross-section survey would overstate the economies of scale.

To summarize, there are many possibilities of distortion and bias that arise from the inadequacies of the data for the inquiry at hand and from attempts to cast them in a form more relevant to the investigation. Chapter 6 contains a more thorough analysis of some of these difficulties, in the light of the statistical analyses that have been conducted and the methods that have been employed.

Next we must take up the problems of statistical methodology which underlie our estimation and testing methods. In studying the cost function, we naturally think of costs Y as being dependent upon several explanatory factors $X_1, X_2, \ldots$, that is,

$$Y = f(X_1, X_2, \ldots, X_k, u)$$

where u denotes a disturbance term, reflecting the stochastic nature of the relationship. Relationships which are linear in the parameters, but not necessarily in the variables, have substantial advantages in that they can adequately describe a wide variety of interdependencies, they are the simplest to handle computationally, and their statistical properties are well known. Thus we may write

$$Y_t = \alpha_0 + \alpha_1 X_{1t} + \alpha_2 X_{2t} + \cdots + \alpha_k X_{kt} + u_t$$
$$(t = 1, 2, \ldots, n) \quad (3\text{-}1)$$

where Y_t represents some measure of "corrected" costs in time t, X_{1t} represents the rate of output in time t, other X's may represent squared or cubed terms in output, and the remaining X's those factors which influence costs but whose effect we want to estimate and then hold constant in order to examine the "net" relationship between costs and output. The problems of statistical inference connected with using (3-1) center around the two related topics of estimation and testing.[1] It is preferable, for example, to use an estimating method which will yield estimators of $\alpha_0, \alpha_1, \ldots, \alpha_k$ possessing desirable properties such as being best, unbiased.[2] Our major concern, however, is with problems of testing various hypotheses about cost-output relationships. For example, three major hypotheses about short-run cost-output variation may be characterized by the inclusion of first-, second-, and third-degree terms in output among the explanatory variables. Analysis of variance tests would then seem an obvious procedure for testing whether the higher-order terms achieve a significant reduction in

[1] For a full discussion of the main problems of statistical inference in econometrics see L. R. Klein, *A Textbook of Econometrics*, Row Peterson & Company, Evanston, Ill., 1953; William C. Hood and Tjalling C. Koopmans, *Studies in Econometric Method*, John Wiley & Sons, Inc., New York, 1953; and Richard Stone, *The Measurement of Consumers' Expenditure and Behavior in the United Kingdom, 1920–1938*, Cambridge University Press, London, 1954, vol. 1, chap. 19.

[2] A best, unbiased estimate is one which, if used repeatedly, would tend to yield a series of estimates whose average would coincide with the true value being estimated and whose variance about that true value is smaller than that of any other unbiased estimate.

the residual variation, or, equivalently, we might test by means of standard error formulas whether the coefficients of the higher-order terms differ significantly from zero. Is the straightforward application of such tests likely to be a valid procedure, when applied to cost-output data?

If we apply least-squares procedure to (3-1) as it stands, we obtain the values $a_0, a_1, \ldots, a_k$, which are such that

$$\sum_{t=1}^{n} (Y_t - a_0 - a_1 X_{1t} - \cdots - a_k X_{kt})^2$$

is minimized. Standard F and t tests are then available to make the tests we require.[1] The strict validity of these tests depends upon the following assumptions:

1. The disturbance is a random normal variable with zero mean for all t. In terms of the cost function this implies that at any given rate of output actual costs will be influenced by very many factors in addition to those actually brought into the relation via $X_1, X_2, \ldots, X_k$. The net effect of these omitted factors is to make costs differ from the value

$$\alpha_0 + \alpha_1 X_1 + \cdots + \alpha_k X_k$$

by positive or negative amounts. These discrepancies are postulated to follow the normal law, so that they are symmetrically distributed about zero and numerically small discrepancies would occur much more frequently than large ones.

2. This normal distribution has constant variance for all t. This implies that the probability of a discrepancy of a given size occurring is independent of the rate of output and is in fact constant all along the cost function. A summary description of this property is *homoscedasticity*. If on the other hand, the probability of discrepancies exceeding a given size increased, say, with the rate of output, we would have heteroscedastic disturbances, and this particular assumption would not be fulfilled.

3. The disturbances are serially independent. For time series data on a given firm this implies that the cost discrepancy in period t is independent of the discrepancies that actually emerged in periods $(t - 1)$, $(t - 2)$, etc. A large positive discrepancy in

[1] See, for example, R. L. Anderson and T. A. Bancroft, *Statistical Theory in Research*, McGraw-Hill Book Company, Inc., New York, 1952, chaps. 13 and 14, or A. M. Mood, *Introduction to the Theory of Statistics*, McGraw-Hill Book Company, Inc., New York, 1950, chap. 13.

period $(t - 1)$ would not create the expectation of a positive discrepancy in period t, just as a head on a given throw of an unbiased coin does not increase the probability of a head on the next throw. If this condition is not fulfilled, we have *autocorrelated* disturbance terms, and this has serious implications for our usual testing procedures.

4. The disturbance is distributed independently of the explanatory variables $X_1, X_2, \ldots, X_k$. Thus, for example, if this assumption is satisfied we should not expect high values of output to be associated, on the average, with, say, positive discrepancies.

The first assumption about the normality of the disturbance term is not of crucial importance, since the tests are not too sensitive to departures from normality.

If the second assumption about homoscedastic disturbances is not fulfilled, then the usual formula for the standard error of a regression coefficient will be inapplicable. For example, in the case of just one explanatory variate,

$$Y = \alpha + \beta X + u \qquad (3\text{-}2)$$

if we denote the least-squares estimate of β by b, the variance of b is given by

$$\text{var } b = E\left(\sum_{t=1}^{n} w_t u_t\right)^2 \qquad (3\text{-}3)$$

where

$$w_t = \frac{x_t}{\sum\limits_{t=1}^{n} x_t^2}$$

the x's denoting deviations from the arithmetic mean of X. In the homoscedastic case we have

$$Eu_t^2 = \sigma^2 \qquad \text{for all } t$$

which, on substitution in (3-3), combined with the assumption of serially independent disturbances, gives

$$\text{var } b = \frac{\sigma^2}{\sum\limits_{t=1}^{n} x_t^2} \qquad (3\text{-}4)$$

Equation (3-3) is perfectly general. It only reduces to the standard textbook equation (3-4) in the special case of a homoscedastic disturbance. If the disturbance is heteroscedastic and we know its form, the correct sampling variance can always be deduced from (3-3) and an appropriate test carried out. For example, if the standard deviation of the disturbance term increases proportionately with the rate of output, we have

$$Eu_t^2 = kX_t^2 \tag{3-5}$$

where k is a constant. On the assumption again of serially independent disturbances we have

$$\text{var } b = \frac{k}{\displaystyle\sum_{t=1}^{n} x_t^2} \cdot \frac{\displaystyle\sum_{t=1}^{n} x_t^2 X_t^2}{\displaystyle\sum_{t=1}^{n} x_t^2} \tag{3-6}$$

The first factor on the right-hand side of (3-6) is reminiscent of the conventional equation (3-4), but the second factor does not appear at all in (3-4). If we do have information about the form of the heteroscedasticity, the most efficient procedure is to use it to effect a transformation of the data before estimating parameters, but a full explanation of this point would take us further into statistical methodology than we can go here. To summarize, heteroscedasticity will render the usual type of variance equation (3-4) incorrect. Little, however, is known, either analytically or as a result of sampling experiments, of the seriousness of the error involved in using the conventional t test, when in fact various degrees of heteroscedasticity are present. It is also frequently difficult to test the assumption of homoscedasticity with the type of cost-output data usually available. If we had several cost observations at each output level we could compute the sample variance about the fitted relation at each output level and test whether these sample variances differed significantly from one another. Cost-output observations are not usually available in replicated form but are usually small in number and scattered with varying density over the output range. A rough test might be obtained by marking off some arbitrary intervals on the output axis, computing the variance about the fitted regression surface within each interval, and testing these variances for homogeneity. The studies described in Chap. 4 had unfortunately to be based on such a small number of observations that it was not considered worthwhile to perform such a rough test.

The autocorrelation problem is potentially serious in all time-series applications, but its presence is much less probable in cross-section studies. Notice that it is the autocorrelation properties of the disturbance term which are involved; the autocorrelation properties of the explanatory variables are not of crucial importance. If the omitted variables, however, are autocorrelated, they will probably impart some autocorrelation to the disturbance term. A second source of such autocorrelation may be an incorrect specification of the functional form. For example, specifying a linear relation in a nonlinear case would yield autocorrelated disturbances about the specified relation. The disturbance is, however, unknown and unobservable, but fortunately a test of its autocorrelation properties is available.[1]

The presence of autocorrelation in the disturbance term has the effect of throwing the conventional standard error formula completely off the mark, and it renders the conventional t and F tests inapplicable. From (3-3) we have

$$\text{var } b = E\left(\sum_{t=1}^{n} w_t u_t\right)^2$$

where

$$w_t = \frac{x_t}{\sum_{t=1}^{n} x_t^2}$$

so that

$$\sum_{t=1}^{n} w_t^2 = \frac{1}{\sum_{t=1}^{n} x_t^2} \quad \text{and} \quad \sum_{t=1}^{n-1} w_t w_{t+1} = \frac{\sum_{t=1}^{n-1} x_t x_{t+1}}{\left(\sum_{t=1}^{n} x_t^2\right)^2}$$

If we make the simplest possible assumption about the autocorrelation of the u's, namely,

$$u_t = \rho u_{t-1} + \epsilon_t \qquad |\rho| < 1 \tag{3-7}$$

where ϵ_t is a random term, substitution in (3-3) will give

$$\text{var } b = \frac{\sigma^2}{\sum_{t=1}^{n} x_t^2}\left(1 + 2\rho\frac{\sum_{t=1}^{n-1} x_t x_{t+1}}{\sum_{t=1}^{n} x_t^2} + 2\rho^2\frac{\sum_{t=1}^{n-2} x_t x_{t+2}}{\sum_{t=1}^{n} x_t^2}\right.$$

$$\left. + \cdots + 2\rho^{n-1}\frac{x_1 x_n}{\sum_{t=1}^{n} x_t^2}\right) \tag{3-8}$$

[1] See J. Durbin and G. S. Watson, "Testing for Serial Correlation in Least-squares Regression," *Biometrika*, I, vol. 37, parts 3 and 4, 1950, pp. 409–423, and II, vol. 38, parts 1 and 2, 1951, pp. 159–178.

where σ^2 denotes the variance of u. If the u's were serially independent, then $\rho = 0$ and (3-8) reduces to the conventional equation (3-4). Inspection of (3-8) reveals that there are two reasons why the conventional formula will give us a very bad estimate of var b. First, it disregards the long term in parentheses on the right-hand side of (3-8). If the X's are positively autocorrelated and if $\rho > 0$, this term will probably exceed unity, thus causing the conventional formula to underestimate the true sampling

TABLE 3-1

ESTIMATION BIAS WITH AUTOCORRELATED DISTURBANCE TERMS

Generating properties of explanatory variable and disturbance term (1)	Number of explanatory variables (2)	Mean variance of residuals (3)	Mean variance of true disturbances (4)
Positively autocorrelated	1	5,142	7,725
Random	1	1,375	1,466
Positively autocorrelated	2 + time	784	4,386
Positively autocorrelated	2	1,690	4,386
Random	2	634	749

SOURCE: D. Cochrane and G. H. Orcutt, "Application of Least-squares Regression to Relationships Containing Auto-correlated Error Terms," *Journal of the American Statistical Association*, vol. 44, no. 245, 1949, p. 52.

variance of b. Secondly, a probably much more serious source of an underestimate from the conventional formula lies in the attempt to estimate σ^2. This is estimated from the residuals about the fitted regression line. With a positively correlated disturbance term and a small number of sample observations, there is quite a high probability of the sample observations clustering in a fairly tight scatter at some remove from the true line. Since the fitting procedure passes a line through the band of *sample* observations, the measured variation about the fitted line will often seriously underestimate the variation of these sample points about the true line. These expectations are confirmed by some sampling experiments of Cochrane and Orcutt,[1] as shown in Table 3-1. Comparison of column (3) with (4) shows the serious underestimate of the

[1] D. Cochrane and G. H. Orcutt, "Application of Least-squares Regression to Relationships Containing Auto-correlated Error Terms," *Journal of the American Statistical Association*, vol. 44, no. 245, 1949, pp. 32–61.

true disturbance variance produced by autocorrelated disturbance terms.

The important practical procedure is to test for the possible presence of autocorrelated disturbances by use of the Durbin-Watson d statistic, before carrying out any conventional significance tests. If it is judged to be present, a suitable transformation of the data should be made to randomize the disturbance and the tests then carried out on the coefficients of the relation between the transformed variables. Attention is paid to this problem in the studies reported in Chap. 4.

Assumption 4 of the linear, normal regression model may often be violated in economic relationships. This assumption requires that the disturbance term in a given relation be distributed independently of the explanatory variables in that relation. Suppose, for example, that we have a partial equilibrium model explaining the equilibrium price and quantity in a given market as the result of the interaction of demand and supply relations. Thus we may write

$$y_{1t} = f^D(y_{2t}, z_{1t}, z_{2t}, u_{1t}) \tag{3-9}$$

$$y_{2t} = f^S(y_{1t}, z_{3t}, z_{4t}, u_{2t}) \tag{3-10}$$

where y_1 denotes price, y_2 quantity, z_1 and z_2 exogenous variables that affect demand, such as the level and distribution of income, z_3 and z_4 are exogenous factors influencing supply, and u_1 and u_2 are disturbance terms. The specification of an exogenous factor is that there is just one-way traffic between the exogenous variables (the z's) and the endogenous variables (the y's), whose values the model is supposed to explain, in the sense that while the z's influence the y's, movements in the latter do *not* feed back and affect the former. Thus national income will affect the price of this commodity, but variations in this price will only have negligible effects on national income; similarly, weather conditions may influence quantity supplied and price, but these will have no influence back upon the weather. Thus a model such as (3-9), (3-10) postulates that the values taken on by y_1 and y_2 are determined jointly by the values taken on by the z's, the u's, and by the precise functional form of the demand and supply relations. This may be brought out explicitly by solving (3-9) and (3-10) for y_1 and y_2 to obtain

$$y_1 = f_1(z_1, z_2, z_3, z_4, u_1, u_2) \tag{3-11}$$

$$y_2 = f_2(z_1, z_2, z_3, z_4, u_1, u_2) \tag{3-12}$$

The assumptions about the z's ensure that they are independent of the u's, but (3-11) and (3-12) clearly express the dependence of the y's on the u's. In particular it is clear that y_2 will, in general, be influenced not only by u_2 but also by u_1. Thus the application of least squares to estimate the parameters of (3-9) would violate one of the basic assumptions of the method since an explanatory variable y_2 is not independent of the disturbance term.

TABLE 3-2

LEAST-SQUARES ESTIMATION OF THE PARAMETERS OF A STRUCTURAL RELATION CONTAINING ENDOGENOUS VARIABLES

	Parameter				
	β_{12}	β_{13}	γ_{11}	γ_{15}	γ_{16}
True value, θ	-2.00000	1.50000	3.00000	-0.60000	10.00000
Mean of 200 L.S. estimates, $\bar{X}$	-0.89358	1.13205	2.33047	-0.58510	-10.68836
$Z = \dfrac{(\bar{X} - \theta)\sqrt{200}}{S}$	15.5119	22.7200	9.1015	2.1746	1.9471
$\Pr\{|\zeta| \geq Z\}$	$<10^{-15}$	$<10^{-15}$	$<10^{-15}$	0.0296	0.0515

SOURCE: R. L. Basmann, "An Experimental Investigation of Some Small Sample Properties of (GCL) Estimators of Structural Equations: Some Preliminary Results," General Electric Company, Richland, Wash., Nov. 21, 1958, p. 83. (Unpublished paper.)

The main effect of this interdependence between explanatory variable and disturbance term is to make the direct application of least squares to the equation yield biased estimates of the parameters of the relation. Furthermore the bias cannot be made negligible, no matter how large the sample becomes; that is, the direct least-squares estimates are both biased and inconsistent. Some sampling studies have shown that the bias may be so great as almost always to lead to the rejection of the hypothesis that the parameter value is θ, where θ is the true value of the parameter. This result is illustrated in Table 3-2.

The βs indicate coefficients of the endogenous variables, and γs coefficients of the exogenous variables. Least squares yields biased estimates of all parameters, but the biases are more serious for the coefficients of the endogenous variables. The Z value in the third line of the table gives the discrepancy between the mean of 200 least-squares estimates and the true value, expressed in standard error units, and the fourth line gives the probability of obtaining a Z value as large in absolute magnitude as that on the line above, given that the hypothesis that the estimator is unbiased is valid. Thus least squares would almost certainly lead us to reject the truth, as being inconsistent with the data.

It is thus very important to establish whether this difficulty is likely to be present in statistical estimation of the cost function. To do this we must spell out the economic decision model which we presume to have generated the observations. Here we encounter the difficulty that the models which have been studied intensively in economic theory may not relate very closely to conditions in the industries for which we have data. However, the statistical principles involved and the possible relevance of various theoretical models may be elucidated by working through a few cases.

Consider first the model of a firm in a perfectly competitive industry. It cannot influence the market price by variation in its own output, and it is assumed to adjust its output in an attempt to maximize short-run profits. The traditional theory is a static equilibrium one, and does not specify the path that the firm will trace out over time; accounting data, however, record such paths for discrete time periods. Thus we need to imagine time divided into discrete planning periods, which we hope would coincide with the accounting periods. We could then specify a production plan being prepared for each period in the light of current conditions and expectations about the future. A simple model might be written formally as

$$P_t^* = P_{t-1} \tag{3-13}$$

$$\Pi_t = \beta_0 + \beta_1 x_t + \beta_2 x_t^2 + u_t \tag{3-14}$$

$$x_t = \frac{1}{2\beta_2} P_{t-1} - \frac{\beta_1}{2\beta_2} + v_t \tag{3-15}$$

where x_t = output in period t

Π_t = total costs in period t

P_{t-1} = market price in period $(t-1)$

P_t^* = market price expected to rule in period t

u_t and v_t = disturbance terms

This model relates to the decision made at the end of period $(t-1)$ about production in the forthcoming period t. Relation (3-13) states that the ruling market price is expected to continue. Relation (3-14) specifies the cost function, which is written as a second-degree polynomial in output, since a linear total cost function is incompatible with perfect competition assumptions. The disturbance term u_t in the cost function implies that costs may vary in a random fashion from period to period about the expected value given by the polynomial. Equation (3-15) reflects the production, or profit-maximizing, decision, stating that the output level x_t is selected at which marginal costs ($\beta_1 + 2\beta_2 x_t$) are equal to expected price ($P_t{}^*$). This gives a planned output

$$x_t{}^* = \frac{1}{2\beta_2} P_{t-1} - \frac{\beta_1}{2\beta_2}$$

Since it is most unlikely that the firm will achieve exactly the desired output, period by period, we add a disturbance term v_t to $x_t{}^*$ and obtain (3-15) as written.

If market price remained constant from period to period as a consequence of no material change in the total demand and supply position of the industry, then very little variation in the output of the firm would be observed, since the only possible source of output variation would be random disturbances about the unique profit-maximizing position. In such a case no method of estimation could give reliable estimates of the parameters of the cost function. If market price varied from period to period, this difficulty would be substantially overcome, but the price-forecasting relation (3-13) would then be unrealistic and would need modification. If the modification took the form of including more information on previous price levels, it would not upset the conclusions reached below about estimation procedures.

The model essentially consists of the two relations (3-14) and (3-15) in the two endogenous variables Π_t and x_t. If u_t is randomly distributed with zero mean and constant variance, the only important remaining assumption for the use of least-squares estimation of the parameters of the cost function is the independence of u and x. Using (3-15), we have

$$Ex_t u_t = \frac{1}{2\beta_2}(P_{t-1} - \beta_1)Eu_t + Eu_t v_t$$

$$= Eu_t v_t$$

Thus u_t will be independent of x_t if u_t is independent of v_t. In general

$$Ex_{t+\tau}u_t = Ev_{t+\tau}u_t \qquad \tau = 0, \pm 1, \pm 2, \ldots$$

The valid application of least squares to the cost function in this model thus rests on the independence of the disturbance terms in the cost function and in the output-determination function. This may not be a very likely result. A disturbance, such as a machine breakdown, which pushes output below a planned level, may push costs above the level expected for the reduced rate of output and thus an inverse relationship between v_t and u_t would hold. Ideally the factors influencing cost variations in various types of output-disturbing situations should be carefully examined, if possible, for each firm subjected to statistical analysis. If the assumption of independence for u and v were valid, then the least-squares estimates of the parameters of the cost function would also be maximum-likelihood estimates. This result is due to the postulated independence and to the fact that the Jacobian of the transformation from u_t, v_t to Π_t, x_t is unity.

$$J = \frac{\partial(u_t, v_t)}{\partial(\Pi_t, x_t)} = \begin{vmatrix} 1 & -\beta_1 - 2\beta_2 \\ 0 & 1 \end{vmatrix} = 1$$

Essentially similar results emerge from a consideration of the orthodox imperfect competition model. Let us assume that the firm has a forecast of the demand function for its product in the forthcoming period, say

$$P_t = \alpha_0 - \alpha_1 x_t$$

giving a forecast total revenue function

$$R_t = \alpha_0 x_t - \alpha_1 x_t^2$$

Assuming, for purposes of exposition, a linear total cost function

$$\Pi_t = \beta_0 + \beta_1 x_t + u_t \tag{3-16}$$

the profit-maximizing rule would give output as

$$x_t = \frac{\alpha_0 - \beta_1}{2\alpha_1} + v_t \tag{3-17}$$

where v_t again denotes the discrepancy between actual and planned output. Using (3-16) and (3-17), we have again

$$Ex_t u_t = Eu_t v_t$$

and if these disturbances are mutually independent, least-squares estimates of the parameters of the cost function would also be maximum-likelihood estimates.

At the present stage of the development of economics we cannot pronounce with any certainty upon the principles governing entrepreneurial decisions. But the two models considered so far have many obvious defects. The perfect competition assumptions are of limited practical relevance, and in the imperfect competition model it is difficult to see where variations in output would come from, unless the firm's demand curve is subject to substantial shifts. This, however, is probably the case, as the demand curve will be affected by many factors outside the direct control of the individual firm, such as the behavior of competitors, changes in consumer tastes, and so on. Once we admit this it seems unlikely that firms will try to estimate the *parameters* of a demand function and base their price-output decisions, period by period, on such imperfectly estimated parameters. For many manufactured products prices do not fluctuate to the extent that such a model would imply. In practice another factor, which does not appear in either of the above models, bears the brunt of shaky sales forecasts, namely, inventories. A realistic model describing the firm's short-run output decision would have to embody major elements such as

1. The formation of the sales forecast
2. The calculation of target or desired inventory levels
3. The discrepancy between current, actual, and target inventory positions
4. The rate at which such discrepancies are planned to be eliminated, taking into consideration such factors as the desirability of fairly stable employment levels, the costs of hiring and firing, future market prospects, both for raw materials and finished products, etc.

Such a model would then give the planned output as a function primarily of forecast sales, target inventory, and actual inventory on hand.

This might be a more realistic type of model to use if we were interested in studying the complex of short-run, production, sales, and inventory decisions. For the narrower problem of studying the cost function the statistical implications of this model are the same as in the previous two cases. If the output level is a function of predetermined variables, such as past levels of sales and inventories, or of arbitrary variables, such as target inventory positions, then the strict requirement for the application of least squares to the cost function is independence of the disturbance terms in the output-determining equation and in the cost function. Less strictly, if we assume no such independence but if discrepancies between planned and actual output are small and if this is only one of the many factors causing disturbances in the cost function, then it is probable that little appreciable dependence between the disturbance and the output term in the cost function will develop. With this qualification, and paying attention also to problems of autocorrelation, least squares may be used in the analysis of the cost-output relation. The empirical studies described in Chap. 4 contain tests of the autocorrelation hypothesis and such information as could be obtained on the principles of output determination; one study also illustrates a check on the assumption of independence of the disturbances in the output determining function and the cost function.

4

Empirical Results

Section 4-1. Electricity Generation

THE DATA

The annual volumes of *Engineering and Financial Statistics* (formerly published by the Electricity Commissioners and continued for a while by the British Ministry of Fuel and Power) give details of output, costs, and revenue for over 500 separate undertakings. It is not possible, however, to derive valid cost functions from these data for the complete process of electricity supply up to the consumption by final consumers on their domestic or business premises. This is because the vast majority of undertakers purchase their electricity in bulk from the national grid and merely act as distributors. Their classified working expenses therefore consist largely of the cost of "wholesale" purchases of electricity, and the derivation, say, of a steadily falling average cost curve from these figures would only reflect the incidence of the two-part grid tariff. Over 100 undertakings, however, generate electricity for the grid, formerly under the directions of the Central Electricity Board and then under the British Electricity Authority. The working costs and units generated each year are recorded separately in each firm's accounts, as are also similar data for those undertakers who still generate part or even all of the electricity required by their customers, so that it is possible to derive valid cost functions for the generation of electricity; the 40 functions derived in this section are all of that type.

44

We considered it desirable to concentrate attention on undertakings which, in 1946–1947, were generating under the directions of the Central Electricity Board:

1. Because such firms are likely to exhibit a much greater variety of output levels than one generating solely to meet the needs of consumption in its own area, or one which is merely producing a small fraction of its total requirements.

2. Because they are likely to represent roughly the best level of performance capable of attainment in the industry.

TABLE 4-1

RELATION OF SAMPLE TO TOTAL NUMBER OF GENERATING STATIONS IN INDUSTRY, 1946–1947

Size of station (installed capacity), kilowatts	No. of stations in industry (public authorities and companies)	No. in sample
150,000 and over	19	8
100,000 but under 150,000	22	8
50,000 but under 100,000	41	6
25,000 but under 50,000	32	4
20,000 but under 25,000	14	3
15,000 but under 20,000	15	4
10,000 but under 15,000	18	1
5,000 but under 10,000	33	6
Under 5,000	157	0
Totals	351	40

The relation of the sample chosen to the total number of generating stations in the industry in 1946–1947 is shown in Table 4-1. The 157 firms in the smallest category were quantitatively very unimportant: over 100 of them had an installed capacity of less than 1,000 kilowatts. On the other hand, the 114 largest stations with an installed capacity each of 25,000 kilowatts or over contained 90.5 per cent of the total plant installed. About 150 of the total number of stations were generating under the directions of the CEB in 1946–1947 and they and the CEB together produced 96.8 per cent of the total output of electricity in that year. Our sample thus constitutes about one-ninth of the total number of generating stations in the industry and about a quarter of the important group of firms generating under the direction of the CEB.

For each undertaking in the sample we extracted the information shown in Table 4-2 from the returns for each year back to 1927–1928, if possible. All undertakings in the sample had steam turbine plant, of which the vast majority consisted of a-c sets. This was the predominating type of plant in use in the industry in 1946–1947, accounting for 96.44 per cent of the total equipment

TABLE 4-2

FIRM 15

Year ended 31 March	Installed capacity, kilowatts (a-c plant)	Thousands of units generated	Working costs of generation, pounds			Total working costs, pounds
			Fuel	Salaries and wages	Repairs and maintenance	
(1)	(2)	(3)	(4)	(5)	(6)	(7)
1947	6,750	4,932	£12,802	£1,983	£3,381	£18,166
1946	6,750	1,760	5,225	1,004	3,268	9,497
.	.	.	.	.	.	.
.	.	.	.	.	.	.
.	.	.	.	.	.	.
.	.	.	.	.	.	.
.	.	.	.	.	.	.
.	.	.	.	.	.	.
1928	6,750	8,727	8,841	7,071†		15,912

† Breakdown not available prior to 1932–1933.

installed. The figures of installed capacity in column (2) of Table 4-2 enable us to classify our sample of 40 firms into two categories: those whose capital equipment remained constant in size and those with changes in capital equipment.

For 17 firms the size of capital equipment remained constant throughout the period; these firms fulfill, therefore, the basic condition of short-period analysis, and for them we may attempt to derive short-period cost functions. It is perhaps conceivable that the constancy of the figure for installed capacity could conceal a change in capital equipment, such as occurs when an old generator set is replaced by a new one of identical capacity but greater thermal efficiency. There are no means of detecting from the published statistics whether this has happened or not, and we have assumed that it is the original equipment which has remained in use. This assumption is likely to be realized in practice since the average life of a generator set is more than 20 years, and it is likely that the capacity of new sets installed will usually be greater than that of the sets they replace. In some of the 17 cases the level of installed capacity did in fact change in the early years of the period 1927–1928 to 1946–1947. Where this occurred we omitted the annual observations in question in order to confine the data to those years in which capital equipment had remained constant. This reduced the number of observations to below 20 in 13 cases.[1]

For each of the remaining 23 firms of the sample, there were several changes of capital equipment in the period studied, and for these we attempt to derive long-run cost functions.

The unit of output is the kilowatthour, and the output of each station is recorded as in column (3) of Table 4-2. The working costs of generation are divided into the three categories of:

1. Fuel, which includes not only the delivered cost of coal but also the handling charges at the station.

2. Salaries and Wages. This item covers only the staff engaged on operation. The salaries and wages incurred in fuel handling or in repairs and maintenance are included under those respective headings.

3. Repairs and Maintenance, Oil, Water, and Stores. This item, as mentioned above, includes the salaries and wages of men engaged on repairs and maintenance. From 1932 to 1947 this category accounted for just over 50 per cent of the costs in this group. The remainder consists of the costs of a wide variety of materials, the more important being boiler tubes and other iron and steel products, lubricating and transformer oil, bricks, cement, electric cables, and paint.

Clearly these three categories, which add up to give the working costs of generation, do not correspond exactly with the variable costs of economic theory. They probably include some element of fixed cost; for example, a certain amount of fuel is required to keep the plant banked ready for operation, and some expenditure on maintenance would likewise be required at zero output. This is borne out by the 40 regression analyses below, all of which have a constant positive term on the right-hand side. This does not affect the derivation of marginal cost functions, since their shape and

[1] See Table 4-3, col. (2).

TABLE 4-3

INSTALLED CAPACITY AND OUTPUT RANGE FOR 17 "SHORT-PERIOD" FIRMS

Firm no.	No. of observations, years	Installed capacity, kw (constant)	Output range, million units	Coefficient of variation of output $= \dfrac{100\sigma}{\bar{x}}$, per cent
(1)	(2)	(3)	(4)	(5)
1	12	1,000 d-c	0.3–8.1	59.8
		8,600 a-c		
2	15	5,500 a-c	0.02–13.1	101.2
3	19	18,125 a-c	12.2–32.1	26.6
4	18	29,750 a-c	12.9–53.4	31.8
5	15	110,000 a-c	181.1–505.7	30.8
6	20	23,750 a-c	21.5–41.6	19.7
7	17	50,000 a-c	42.7–97.0	23.1
8	19	23,300 a-c	18.8–54.7	31.1
9	18	17,500 a-c	16.7–62.4	29.1
10	15	15,350 a-c	8.4–23.0	33.5
11	20	15,250 a-c	7.9–50.8	40.8
		750 d-c		
12	18	4,375 a-c	3.4–10.3	33.7
		9,000 d-c		
13	19	85,000 a-c	53.3–129.8	21.7
14	14	37,000 a-c	45.3–126.5	27.4
15	20	6,750 a-c	0.5–19.7	103.6
16	20	29,750 a-c	2.8–42.9	87.4
17	18	7,500 a-c	0.6–12.5	66.7

position are not influenced by the level of fixed costs and they may equally well be derived from the true total variable cost function or from any function found by adding a constant term to the total variable cost function.

The statistical returns, unfortunately, are not so helpful with respect to capital costs. It is impossible to deduce from them the capital charges associated with any given plant level, or the variations in such charges as the scale of plant is varied. Each return up to and including 1937–1938 does give figures of "Expenditure charged to capital account" subdivided between (1) Land, Buildings, and Civil Engineering Works and (2) Plant and Machinery, but these are purely historical costs reflecting the total expenditure on each category in the life of the undertaking. The plant and machinery figure, for example, may be the sum total of the initial

TABLE 4-4

INSTALLED CAPACITY AND OUTPUT RANGE FOR 23 "LONG-PERIOD" FIRMS

Firm no.	No. of observations, years	Range of installed capacity, kw (a-c)	Output range, million units	Coefficient of variation of output, per cent
(1)	(2)	(3)	(4)	(5)
18	20	69,500–120,000	107.5–308.4	35.1
19	20	21,000–45,000	7.5–165.4	103.6
20	20	14,700–86,900	15.7–363.4	104.3
21	16	9,000–13,000	4.3–43.5	59.6
22	20	61,250–132,500	124.0–561.8	41.3
23	14	140,000–345,000	100.4–1,561.3	34.2
24	15	100,000–165,700	196.0–531.0	20.6
25	15	106,750–117,250	67.2–416.1	47.8
26	15	50,000–140,000	101.6–636.6	43.2
27	15	156,250–131,250	82.5–324.6	43.1
28	20	25,000–95,000	26.0–353.4	113.9
29	20	35,400–87,500	47.5–437.8	93.7
30	20	155,250–238,500	216.5–790.8	42.3
31	15	37,500–130,750	59.0–376.8	52.0
32	15	169,000–222,000	372.1–727.4	15.3
33	15	64,875–168,075	174.0–1,021.8	44.1
34	15	25,000–185,000	3.9–920.5	59.6
35	15	122,500–178,000	446.0–881.5	20.9
36	15	90,000–244,500	188.4–1,437.2	43.1
37	20	46,500–76,250	36.7–279.4	74.6
38	20	24,000–125,000	35.7–539.7	59.5
39	20	13,000–20,750	10.8–44.9	33.3
40	20	10,250–9,000	1.7–17.3	69.2

costs of several different items of plant and cannot be taken as the specific cost of the current equipment. This difficulty is of no importance in the short-run analysis since we are interested primarily in the shape of the cost functions and not in their absolute level. For the long-run analysis, however, an attempt will have to be made to estimate the nature of the variation in capital charges as output (and plant scale) vary.

Tables 4-3 and 4-4 give the more important features of the 40 sample firms. The firms have been numbered from 1 to 40 for convenience of reference. Column (2) shows in both tables the number of annual observations from which the cost function for each firm will be derived. The maximum number of observations in any case is 20, and the average for the 40 firms is just over 17. This is admittedly rather small, but could not be avoided in the present study for three reasons:

1. It was not possible to obtain price index numbers for the three categories of working costs extending back over a longer period.

2. In working with annual data, the attempt to increase the number of observations increased the possibility of important changes in techniques, and so forth, having occurred in the longer period studied. Thus a balance had to be struck between the desire for a large number of observations and a short time period.

3. Care had to be taken to obtain a sufficient number of firms, which would conform to the requirement of having had constant capital equipment. This led in 13 out of 17 cases to a smaller number of years than the maximum 20 (Table 4-3).

On the other hand, taking a fairly large sample of firms will enable us to detect the existence of any uniformity in the type of cost function found, and will to some extent compensate for the small number of observations in individual cases.

Column (3) gives the installed capacity of each station, which is, of course, constant for the 17 firms in Table 4-3. The corresponding figures in Table 4-4 show the highest and lowest levels of installed capacity in the remaining 23 firms. The range of installed capacity is not usually as great as would be theoretically desirable for a good approximation to the long-run cost function, which is supposed to cover a very large number of plant scales. In a few cases the highest plant level is as much as five, six, or seven times as great as the lowest level, but in most cases the ratio is about 2 :1. A further drawback to the available statistical data is the fact that the different plant scales do not necessarily refer to different sets of plant; for example, in expanding from a capacity of, say, 50,000 to 80,000 kilowatts, a firm may retain all its existing equipment and merely install an extra 30,000 kilowatts of new plant. This will not seriously vitiate the statistical approximation to the long-run cost function if the existing equipment tends to be just as efficient as new equipment of equal capacity. On account of both of these difficulties, however, it is desirable to supplement these 23 estimates of the long-run cost function with a few additional estimates derived from "cross-section" studies.

The latter method raises difficulties of its own. The variation of costs from firm to firm in a given year may be due not solely to different output levels and plant scales but also to differences in the type, age, and obsolescence of plant, nearness to coal fields, efficiency of management, etc. It is, however, possible to take a large sample of firms in cross-section studies and trust that the large numbers will to some extent result in an averaging out of these diverse effects.

Finally, column (4) of Tables 4-3 and 4-4 shows the range of output for each firm, and column (5) the coefficient of variation computed for output to give a relative measure of the dispersion of output in the different firms of the sample.

METHOD OF ANALYSIS

There are two main problems involved in the derivation of cost functions from raw data. The first is the rectification of the data to remove the influence upon costs of all factors other than output. As a recent writer[1] says, the cost function

... is a *ceteris paribus* proposition that demands an intricate processing of the normally available accounting data, if these are to yield the hidden relationship which the cost function represents.

After this processing, the second problem is the purely statistical one of how best to estimate the relationship existing between cost and output.

1. *Processing the Data.* Each of the three cost categories was deflated with an appropriate price index number. This procedure strictly involves two assumptions: first, that changes in relative factor prices have not resulted in any substitution between those factors in the productive process, and second, that changes in the firm's output have not had any influence upon factor prices. The first assumption is obviously justified since men are a poor substitute for coal in the generation of electricity and vice versa, and the second seems equally reasonable, except perhaps in the case of the very largest firms.

The factor price index numbers employed[2] are shown in Table 4-5. Index *A* is based on the average cost of fuel to generating

---

[1] Hans Apel, "Marginal Cost Constancy and Its Implications," *American Economic Review*, vol. 38, no. 5, 1948, p. 870.

[2] L. O'Donnell, economic adviser to the British Electricity Authority, has kindly supplied index numbers *A*, *B*, and *C*.

TABLE 4-5

FACTOR PRICE INDEX NUMBERS FOR USE AS DEFLATORS

Year	A, inclusive fuel cost (1938 = 100)	B, calorific value of coal (1938 = 100)	$A' = A \div B$	C, average earnings (1938–1939 = 100)	D, equal weights given to C and prices of industrial materials (1938 = 100)
(1)	(2)	(3)	(4)	(5)	(6)
1946	224.5	94.3	238.1	162.7	170.4
1945	215.2	95.2	226.1	151.2	160.0
1944	190.8	96.3	198.1	167.4	166.0
1943	170.5	98.0	174.0	161.5	159.9
1942	159.8	98.4	162.4	158.1	156.4
1941	147.7	98.8	149.5	139.0	144.7
1940	124.0	99.1	125.1	130.3	132.0
1939	105.4	99.8	105.6	130.3	116.1
1938	100.0	100.0	100.0	100.0	100.0
1937	88.0	98.5	90.2	93.3	100.8
1936	76.4	98.0	78.0	94.2	93.3
1935	72.9	97.4	74.8	94.1	90.6
1934	68.4		68.4	93.9	90.0
1933	73.3		73.3	93.7	88.8
1932	76.3		76.3	95.1	89.5
1931	75.3†		75.3	95.1	
1930	73.6		73.6	98.1	
1929	74.3		74.3	99.5	
1928	70.1		70.1	100.9	
1927	79.0		79.0	104.4	

† BEA figures are only available down to 1932. Figures for the 5 years 1927–1931 were found by taking a simple average of coal price relatives based on the prices quoted in *United Kingdom Statistical Abstract* 78, Command Paper 4801, pp. 224–225, and splicing this series on to the BEA index. Extension of this simple average of price relatives for the years 1932–1938 showed that it corresponded much more closely with the BEA index for these years than either of the two alternatives of (1) a simple aggregative price index, and (2) the coal subgroup of the Board of Trade index of wholesale prices, which were also tried.

stations, including handling charges. Index B is an index of the calorific value of coal. A new index A' ($= A/B$) has been formed and used to deflate the original fuel cost series for each firm. This gives the value of the fuel consumed in each year stabilized at 1938 average prices and average calorific value. The B index, unfortunately, is not available prior to 1935, but it is probable that the changes in quality since the base year 1938 are greater than those in the thirties. Index C is an index of the average annual earnings of all persons engaged in regular employment in maintaining and operating electricity undertakings. It therefore covers more than the earnings of those employees solely on generation work, but it does not seem likely that any differential between the earnings of (1) employees concerned with generation alone and (2) the other employees of electricity undertakings has altered appreciably during the period studied. Index C has therefore been used to deflate the second category of working costs, Salaries and Wages.

Index D has been formed by combining with equal weights the index of average earnings (C) and the Board of Trade's index for the prices of industrial materials, and has then been employed to deflate the third cost category, Repairs and Maintenance, Oil, Water, and Stores. This separation between the second and third cost categories is only available since 1932. For the earlier years the working costs of generation were simply divided in the returns into (1) Fuel Costs and (2) Other Costs. Ideally, therefore, a new index should be constructed for the deflation of Other Costs in the 5 years 1927–1931. Since Salaries and Wages and Repairs and Maintenance, Oil, Water, and Stores are in many cases of roughly the same size, and since labor costs constitute about 50 per cent of the latter category, the new index should be weighted three-quarters Average Earnings and one-quarter Prices of Industrial Materials. Because of the predominating weight of Average Earnings and the fact that for many of the sample firms there are few or no observations in these 5 years, we have simply used index C alone for the correction of any Other Cost data that appeared.

There are three final difficulties attendant upon the use of these factor price index numbers. All indices relate to calendar years; except C, which relates to fiscal years April 1 to March 31. For simplicity, in combining C with the price index of industrial materials, we have taken each value of C to correspond to the calendar year which contained 9 months of the actual fiscal year, that is, the 1946–1947 figures have been taken to relate to the calendar year 1946, and so on. Secondly, these index numbers have been applied to deflate the cost data of both Public Authority and Company undertakings. The accounting year for the former is April–March and, for the latter, January–December, so that there is not in all cases an exact correspondence between the periods to which the index numbers and the cost data relate—the minimum common period being, of course, 9 months. This, however, is unlikely to affect the trend of the deflated figures, though their absolute value may be, throughout, slightly too high or too low. Thirdly, the common set of deflators has been applied to all 40 sample firms. Ideally a separate set of deflators should be constructed for each firm. But even if the data were readily available, it is doubtful if the enormous labor involved would be justified by the resultant gains in accuracy. When the three cost series had been deflated for each firm, they were summed to give total deflated working costs for each output.

2. *Statistical Estimation of the Cost-Output Relationship.* We have examined in Chap. 3 the appropriate estimation procedure when the firm is assumed to adjust its rate of output in accordance with some principle such as profit maximization, and it was found even then that single-equation least-squares methods would often be appropriate. The situation in electricity generation is even simpler in that the 40 firms in our study were all generating electricity (for the majority of the years studied) at such times and in such quantities as directed by the CEB. Thus they were in no wise in the position of themselves adjusting output in the search for maximum profits, as traditionally assumed in economic theory. Their problem was the single, internal one of minimizing costs for various arbitrary output levels. Thus we may apply single-equation least-squares methods to estimate the parameters of the cost function, treating cost as the dependent variable and output as the independent variable.

The cost functions of economic theory are timeless abstractions, while the data available in empirical research are usually observations from different time periods. Therefore we must proceed on the assumption (1) that the relationship being approximated has remained unchanged during the period studied, or (2) that it has changed in some definable and measurable way. Since there are many different factors making for shifts in the cost function (obsolescence of plant, changed management techniques and production methods, etc.), all of which are not likely to show startling changes in the same year, we may assume that the combined over-all influence of these factors changes slowly and smoothly with time. Thus we include time as an additional explanatory variable in our cost equations.

The method adopted has been to commence by fitting one of the simplest equations of all, that giving total cost Y as a linear function of output X and time T. The term in T was only retained in the regression equation if its coefficient proved, on application of the t test, to be significantly different from zero at the 5 per cent level. A scatter diagram was then drawn for each firm showing "corrected" costs (that is, actual costs with the influence of T removed in those cases where T was retained as an explanatory variable) plotted against output. Where there was any indication of curvilinearity in the scatter, additional terms in X^2 and/or X^3 were brought into the analysis and retained in the final regression if their coefficients differed significantly from zero. A term in X^2 was computed for about two-thirds of the sample firms and proved nonsignificant in more than half these cases. Only a few scatter diagrams indicated that a cubic function might possibly give a better fit, but the improvement was too slight to be significant in any case.

RESULTS

Table 4-6 gives the regression equations and the correlation coefficients for the 17 short-run analyses. From columns (7) and (8) it is seen that the fitted regressions have explained a very high percentage of the total variance in Y, the average figure being 94.1 per cent. Of the 17 regressions, 10 have explained more than 95 per cent of the variance in the cost data, and the fit of the corresponding lines or surfaces to the observed data must be considered very good. The average correlation coefficient is found to be 0.966. In no case is the correlation coefficient below 0.9, while in 12 cases it is greater than 0.95.

The best-fitting regressions are of two main types:

1. Twelve equations contain only a linear term in output X. These 12 cost functions thus yield constant marginal and average variable cost curves, and they correspond to the third type of short-period cost situation specified in Chap. 2. Of these twelve regressions, seven also contain a significant term in T. This latter term is significant at the 10 per cent level in two cases, at the 1 per cent level in two cases, and at the 0.1 per cent level in the remaining three cases. The economic interpretation of a significant term in T is that the cost function is shifting slowly but regularly with the passage of time, the direction and extent of the shift being indicated by the sign and magnitude of the coefficient of T. Of the seven coefficients of T, 5 have a positive sign, indicating a predominance of those factors such as plant obsolescence, etc., making for an increase in costs.

2. Five firms have a quadratic total variable cost function, and

TABLE 4-6

SUMMARY OF SHORT-PERIOD RESULTS

Firm no.	Best-fitting regressions					Percentage of Y variance explained by regression	$\bar{R}$ (or $\bar{r}$)†
	Y'	a	bX	cX^2	dT		
(1)	(2)	(3)	(4)	(5)	(6)	(7)	(8)
1	$Y' =$	3.9	$+2.048X$ $\pm0.111\P$			96.0	0.978
2	$Y' =$	5.1	$+0.958X$ $\pm0.044\P$			97.4	0.986
3	$Y' =$	3.8	$+1.540X$ $\pm0.090\P$			94.5	0.970
4	$Y' =$	16.7	$+1.122X$ $\pm0.097\P$			89.3	0.942
5	$Y' =$	42.4	$+0.634X$ $\pm0.027\P$			97.8	0.988
6	$Y' =$	15.9	$+0.550X$ $\pm0.077\P$		$+0.155T$ ±0.078	83.7	0.904
7	$Y' =$	42.1	$+0.678X$ $\pm0.066\P$		$+0.875T$ $\pm0.224\S$	89.3	0.937
8	$Y' =$	18.3	$+0.889X$ $\pm0.042\P$		$-0.639T$ $\pm0.079\P$	97.4	0.985
9	$Y' =$	16.2	$+0.847X$ $\pm0.049\P$		$+0.485T$ $\pm0.119\P$	96.1	0.978
10	$Y' =$	10.3	$+1.133X$ $\pm0.098\P$		$+0.219T$ ±0.118	91.9	0.952
11	$Y' =$	13.0	$+0.789X$ $\pm0.069\P$		$+0.415T$ $\pm0.112\S$	95.8	0.976
12	$Y' =$	4.6	$+1.046X$ $\pm0.090\P$		$-0.162T$ $\pm0.034\P$	90.2	0.943
13	$Y' =$	20.6	$+2.072X$ $\pm0.527\S$	$-0.0065X^2$ $\pm0.0028\ddagger$	$-2.035T$ $\pm0.323\P$	95.8	0.974
14	$Y' =$	73.2	$-0.579X$ ±0.409	$+0.0065X^2$ $\pm0.0023\ddagger$		88.0	0.926
15	$Y' =$	3.7	$+1.694X$ $\pm0.110\P$	$-0.0427X^2$ $\pm0.0055\P$	$-0.247T$ $\pm0.042\P$	99.1	0.995
16	$Y' =$	17.2	$+2.285X$ $\pm0.257\P$	$-0.0178X^2$ $\pm0.006\S$	$-0.813T$ $\pm0.182\P$	98.6	0.992
17	$Y' =$	3.8	$+2.439X$ $\pm0.231\P$	$-0.058X^2$ $\pm0.018\S$	$-0.307T$ $\pm0.047\P$	98.9	0.993
Average						94.1	0.966

Y = total deflated working expenses, £000 (Y' = regression values).
X = annual output, million units.
T = time, years.
† $\bar{R}$ (or $\bar{r}$) = estimate of the correlation in the population, i.e., sample values of $R(r)$ adjusted for degrees of freedom.
‡ Significant at 5 per cent level.
§ Significant at 1 per cent level.
¶ Significant at 0.1 per cent level.
NOTE: For firms 6 and 10, T is only significant at the 10 per cent level.

all but one of them have a significant term in T as well. In only one of the five cases is the coefficient of X^2 significant at the 0.1 per cent level, while two are significant at the 1 per cent level, and the remaining two at the 5 per cent level. The sign of the X^2 term in four of the five firms is negative, contrary to theoretical expectation, which postulates steadily increasing AVC and MC functions in the case of a quadratic total cost function. A possible explanation of this discrepancy might perhaps be as follows.

Since the output observations usually fall well short of maximum output, the quadratic functions with a negative term in X^2 may be just the first section of the orthodox third-degree polynomial, the second section not being observable in practice. The reasonableness of this hypothesis can only be tested by examining the size of the larger outputs of each firm in relation to its capacity. For this purpose the coefficients of variation shown in Table 4-7 are not sufficient, since they refer to the dispersion of outputs about the mean value, so that it is quite possible for a firm to exhibit a large coefficient of variation and yet have no outputs near peak capacity because of a low average output. Nor are the load factors shown in the *Engineering and Financial Statistics* any help since, in the case of firms generating under the instructions of the CEB, these load factors are based on the firms' distribution activities. Load factors relating specifically to generation are, however, given in a different set of annual returns, *Generation of Electricity in the United Kingdom*. The earlier issues of these are now out of print but an examination of those available (1946, 1945, 1937, 1935, 1933, 1932, 1931, 1930) shows the load factors of the firms in question to be roughly similar to those of the other short-period firms, so it is unlikely that this hypothesis accounts for the negative sign of the term in X^2. Further, if it were merely the first section of the orthodox cubic polynomial, then most of the other firms would be expected to show a similar curvature, since they have equally high outputs in relation to capacity. Taking into consideration, therefore, the small number of firms showing a significant term in X^2, the conflicting signs, and the rather low significance levels of the regression coefficients, the short-period results tend to support the thesis of a linear total cost function with constant AVC and MC functions.

The nature of these curves and the method of their derivation may be better appreciated with the aid of a few graphs. Figure 4-1 illustrates the simplest type of total cost function—a linear regression giving Y in terms of X. Each point of the scatter indicates a given annual output for firm 5 and the associated value of deflated total working expenses. Fitting a simple linear regression of Y upon X gave the equation $Y = 42.4 + 0.634X$ with

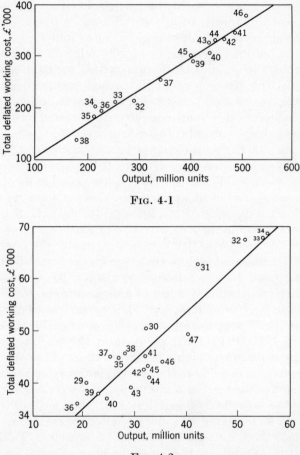

Fig. 4-1

Fig. 4-2

$r^2 = 0.978$; that is, the linear relationship accounts for 97.8 per cent of the variance in the deflated cost figures. In this case the inclusion of terms in T, X^2, or X^3 did not add significantly to the percentage of explained variability, so that the linear equation is taken as our estimate of the cost function.

Figure 4-2 shows the original cost-output scatter diagram for

firm 8. The trend of the scatter is approximately linear, but a simple linear equation only accounted for 86.5 per cent of the variance in Y. Upon examination of the scatter of points about this regression line, it is seen that the observations for the years 1929–1938, inclusive, all lie above the regression line; the observation for 1939 lies exactly upon it, and those for the years 1940–1947 all lie below it. This suggests the existence of a downward trend in costs with the passage of time. Therefore we include T as an additional explanatory variable and fit a multiple linear regression of the general form $Y = a + bX + cT$. This results in the equation

$$Y' = 18.3 + 0.889X - 0.639T$$

Then for each year we compute what cost would have been in the absence of any time trend. This is done by inserting the appropriate value of T in the expression

$$Y + 0.639T$$

where Y denotes the actual deflated cost figures as compared with Y', which represents the values given by the regression equation. The series of values given by $Y + 0.639T$ (in general $Y - cT$) is labeled here "corrected cost" and plotted against output in order to examine more fully the net relationship between cost and output when the influence of time upon the former has been removed. (In all cases the origin of measurement for T has been taken at the center of the period covered by the particular set of observations.) This net scatter is shown in Fig. 4-3. The net linear regression has a somewhat gentler slope than the simple regression of Fig. 4-2. The scatter of observations about the regression, however, is much closer in Fig. 4-3 than in Fig. 4-2, and the inclusion of T in the analysis has in fact raised the percentage of explained variability from 86.5 to 97.4 per cent. There is a very slight suggestion in Fig. 4-3 that a quadratic function in X might give a still better fit. So, as the next step, X^2 was included in the analysis and the partial correlation coefficient between Y and X^2 computed, with X and T held constant. This coefficient was -0.2790, which was shown to be nonsignificant by the use of the t test. Finally, the net scatter gives no indication that a cubic term in X would significantly improve the fit, so the best-fitting cost function is here a linear multiple regression in X and T.

The third type of cost function found is illustrated in Figs. 4-4 and 4-5. Figure 4-4 shows the original scatter with a simple linear regression accounting for 96.3 per cent of the variance in the cost data. The inclusion of T raises this percentage significantly to 97.8 per cent, the partial correlation coefficient being $r_{YT.X} = -0.6365$, which is significant at the 1 per cent level. The net

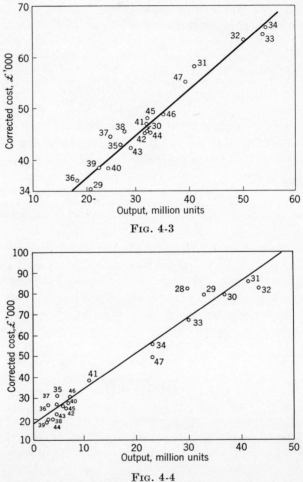

Fig. 4-3

Fig. 4-4

scatter between corrected cost and output is then examined, as above, and X^2 again included. This time the partial coefficient between Y and X^2 with X and T constant is found to be significantly different from zero, and the corresponding multiple curvilinear regression advances the percentage of explained variability

still farther to 98.6 per cent. The net curvilinear regression is
shown in Fig. 4-5.

In addition to visual inspection of the partial scatter diagrams
and the application of the *t* test, a further method of investigating
the fit of a given function to the observed data is to test the "unexplained" residuals for randomness. As pointed out in Chap. 3,
this is also an important test of the validity of the statistical

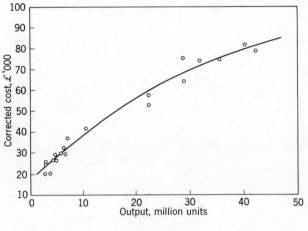

Fɪɢ. 4-5

methods employed, which rest on the assumption of an independent disturbance term. The residuals are the deviations of the
observed *Y* values from the corresponding points on the regression
line or surface. These residuals may then be arranged either in
order of time, or in ascending or descending order of output. If
the fit of the function is satisfactory, both sets of residuals should
be random; that is, successive residuals should not tend to have
like signs. The randomness of the residuals may be tested either
by computing their serial correlation coefficient or by use of the
mean-square successive difference method.[1] These tests were
applied to six of the seventeen firms, taking care to include firm 6,
which had the lowest percentage of explained variability. The
firms tested were numbers 1, 6, 7, 8, 9, and 13. The average percentage of explained variability in these six firms was 93 per cent,

[1] As explained in Chap. 3, the most appropriate test is provided by the
Durbin-Watson *d* statistic.

which is slightly lower than the average of 94.1 per cent for the whole group. For all firms except no. 6, the tests showed both sets of residuals to be random, thus reinforcing the conclusions of the

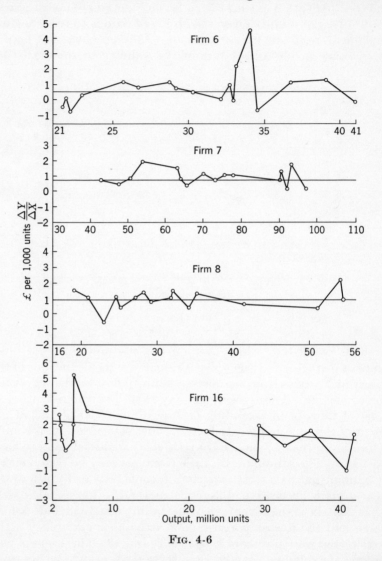

Fig. 4-6

previous tests that the fitted functions give a very good explanation of the observed data and that no important explanatory variable has been omitted.

A valuable test of the marginal cost functions derived from the regression equations is to compare them with the successive values of $\Delta Y / \Delta X$ computed from the cost-output data, where ΔX is the observed change in output (positive or negative) between successive years and ΔY is the corresponding change in cost. Each $\Delta Y / \Delta X$ value may then be plotted against the corresponding value of X, and the resultant series of observations compared with the marginal cost function given by the derivative of the total cost function. Where time has been included in the regression equation, the ΔY values are computed from the series of deflated costs corrected for the influence of time, and the linear marginal cost function is calculated for the middle of the period, that is, where $T = 0$. Substituting different values for T would merely move the marginal cost line up or down without changing its shape. The results of these calculations for 4 of the 17 firms are shown in Fig. 4-6, the broken line joining successive values of $\Delta Y / \Delta X$ and the single straight line showing the derived MC function. In most cases the fit of the computed MC functions to the $\Delta Y / \Delta X$ values is fairly good. This is particularly true for firms 2, 5, 6, 7, 8, 10, and 11. For the first 13 firms also the trend of the $\Delta Y / \Delta X$ values seems approximately linear, in agreement with the computed MC functions. For firm 14, which had a quadratic total cost function and linear, increasing marginal cost, the $\Delta Y / \Delta X$ values suggest constant marginal cost. (The coefficient of X^2 in the regression equation was only significant at the 5 per cent level.) For the remaining 4 firms, nos. 13, 15, 16, and 17, the trend of the $\Delta Y / \Delta X$ figures is in accord with the declining marginal cost functions derived from the regression equations. Thus the two methods of computing marginal cost are in substantial agreement, and in two-thirds of the cases result in constant marginal and average variable cost functions over the observed range of output, which suggests that the prevailing type of short-period cost situation in this industry is the third type outlined in Chap. 2.[1]

---

[1] Professor Champernowne has suggested that while the coefficients of X^2 or X^3 may prove nonsignificant in individual regressions, because of the small number of observations on which each regression is based, it may be possible by considering these coefficients in the aggregate to infer something about the possible curvature of the total cost function. The following table shows the nonsignificant partial correlation coefficients for 10 out of the 12 remaining short-period firms, with the degrees of freedom shown in parentheses.

The Long-period Results

A similar analysis was carried out for the 23 firms whose capital equipment had not remained constant during the period studied. Y, as before, represents total deflated working expenses and X output, but this time the regression of Y upon X is not sufficient to determine the shape of the total cost function, since capital charges will vary as the firm moves from one scale of plant to another.

Examining first of all the regressions of total working expenses on output as shown in Table 4-7, it is seen that the equations fitted have explained an even higher percentage of the Y variance than in the short-period cases. The average percentage is now 97.5 per cent and the average value of $\bar{R}$ is 0.985, while several individual values of each exceed 0.99. Once again the predominating type of equation is a linear function of output, with or without the inclusion of a term in T. Of the equations, 17 are of this type, and the remaining 6 yield quadratic cost functions, while none of the 23 scatter diagrams gave any indication that a cubic function would improve the fit. Of the 17 functions linear in X, only 8

PARTIAL CORRELATION COEFFICIENTS BETWEEN Y AND X^2
(All nonsignificant at the 5 per cent level)

Positive coefficients	*Negative coefficients*
0.3933 (14)†	−0.0964 (17)
0.3379 (8)	−0.1399 (14)
0.0646 (12)	−0.2790 (15)
0.1475 (12)	−0.4539 (12)
	−0.0167 (15)
	−0.2513 (14)

† Degrees of freedom shown in parentheses

In the case of the other two firms, it was obvious from inspection of the net scatter diagrams that a second- or third-degree function would give a worse fit than the linear regression and so no additional terms were computed. For one of the above ten firms, the scatter gives a slight indication that a cubic function might improve the fit. The partial correlation coefficient between Y and X^3 was 0.1512 (11), again nonsignificant. Considering significant and nonsignificant coefficients together for the 15 short-period firms then yields a total cost function with negative curvature (*MC* decreasing) in 10 cases, and positive curvature (*MC* increasing) in 5 cases. Thus two-thirds of the coefficients have the opposite sign to that expected in the conventional theory, and two-thirds of them are also not significantly different from zero.

TABLE 4-7

SUMMARY OF LONG-PERIOD RESULTS

Firm no.	Best-fitting regressions					Percentage of Y variance explained by regression	$\bar{R}$ (or $\bar{r}$)
	Y'	a	bX	cX^2	dT		
(1)	(2)	(3)	(4)	(5)	(6)	(7)	(8)
18	$Y' =$	71.5	$+0.588X$ $\pm0.029\S$			95.8	0.978
19	$Y' =$	13.6	$+0.645X$ $\pm0.016\S$			98.9	0.994
20	$Y' =$	16.9	$+0.647X$ $\pm0.010\S$			99.6	0.998
21	$Y' =$	4.5	$+1.063X$ $\pm0.034\S$			98.6	0.992
22	$Y' =$	72.7	$+0.546X$ $\pm0.034\S$			93.4	0.965
23	$Y' =$	28.3	$+0.570X$ $\pm0.028\S$			97.3	0.985
24	$Y' =$	96.9	$+0.693X$ $\pm0.050\S$			93.6	0.965
25	$Y' =$	109.5	$+0.543X$ $\pm0.038\S$			94.4	0.969
26	$Y' =$	21.6	$+0.602X$ $\pm0.013\S$			99.4	0.996
27	$Y' =$	77.0	$+1.316X$ $\pm0.212\S$	$-0.00133X^2$ $\pm0.000516\dagger$		97.9	0.988
28	$Y' =$	15.3	$+0.613X$ $\pm0.016\S$		$-0.672T$ $\pm0.248\dagger$	99.3	0.996
29	$Y' =$	46.3	$+0.499X$ $\pm0.018\S$		$+1.155T$ $\pm0.380\ddagger$	99.2	0.996
30	$Y' =$	207.1	$+0.348X$ $\pm0.120\ddagger$		$+11.028T$ $\pm4.356\dagger$	91.4	0.951
31	$Y' =$	54.7	$+0.671X$ $\pm0.033\S$		$+6.101T$ $\pm0.827\S$	99.6	0.998
32	$Y' =$	35.9	$+1.147X$ $\pm0.306\ddagger$	$-0.00069X^2$ $\pm0.00027\dagger$	$+14.173T$ $\pm1.438\S$	98.8	0.992
33	$Y' =$	99.1	$+0.442X$ $\pm0.028\S$		$+6.754T$ $\pm3.417\ddagger$	99.6	0.998
34	$Y' =$	115.6	$+0.375X$ $\pm0.035\S$		$+15.736T$ $\pm2.488\S$	99.6	0.997
35	$Y' =$	192.8	$+0.481X$ $\pm0.034\S$		$+5.226T$ $\pm1.143\S$	96.0	0.976
36	$Y' =$	112.7	$+0.539X$ $\pm0.022\S$		$+16.751T$ $\pm1.964\S$	99.4	0.996
37	$Y' =$	24.4	$+0.973X$ $\pm0.053\S$	$-0.0012X^2$ $\pm0.0002\S$		99.8	0.999
38	$Y' =$	144.4	$+0.153X$ ±0.152	$+0.0005X^2$ $\pm0.0002\dagger$	$+1.832T$ $\pm1.864\S$	97.4	0.984
39	$Y' =$	35.3	$-0.640X$ ±0.458	$+0.0300X^2$ $\pm0.0080\ddagger$	$+0.525T$ $\pm0.133\ddagger$	93.5	0.961
40	$Y' =$	9.4	$+0.591X$ ±0.410	$+0.1092X^2$ $\pm0.0230\S$	$-0.240T$ $\pm0.094\dagger$	98.5	0.991
Average						97.5	0.985

† Significant at 5 per cent level.
‡ Significant at 1 per cent level.
§ Significant at 0.1 per cent level.

have an additional term in T. The sign of the latter term is positive in all cases except one, thus once again indicating the preponderance of those factors making for a rise in costs with the passage of time. (Alternatively it is perhaps possible that the average index numbers used failed to correct fully for rising factor prices in all the firms in the sample.)

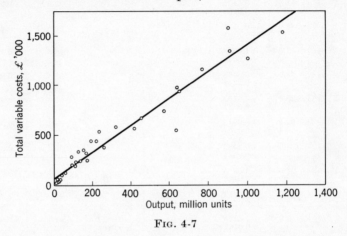

Fig. 4-7

This linear relationship between total working costs and output is strongly supported by two cross-section studies. The first is based on a sample of 40 firms for the year 1946–1947, with outputs ranging from 1.1 to 1,150.5 million units. The simple linear regression was

$$Y' = 57.6 + 1.3928X$$

with $r^2 = 0.9534$ and $r = 0.9764$. The scatter and regression lines are shown in Fig. 4-7, and the terms in X^2 and X^3 are both nonsignificant.[1]

[1] Data on thermal efficiency are available for 35 of the 40 cross-section firms for the year 1946–1947. So a second analysis was tried in which thermal efficiency was included as an additional explanatory variable, in order to take account of differences in the age, type, and efficiency of different plants. The relationship fitted was the logarithmic form

$$Y' = AX^{\alpha}e^{\beta V}$$

where V = thermal efficiency, per cent. This form of equation was chosen since a given change in V may be expected to exert a constant proportional change, rather than a constant absolute change, in Y. The fitted equation was

$$Y' = 8.301X^{0.7919}e^{-0.0175V}$$

A similar analysis of 33 firms in 1938–1939 gives another linear regression and no evidence of curvilinearity, with $r^2 = 0.9758$ and $r = 0.9878$. These data are shown in Fig. 4-8. There seems little doubt, therefore, that the relationship of total variable costs to

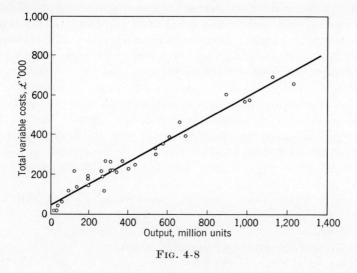

FIG. 4-8

with $R^2 = 0.9878$ and $R = 0.9939$. Holding V constant at its average level of 19.54 per cent for the 35 firms gives an alternative estimate of average variable cost

$$AVC = \frac{Y'}{X} = 5.8956X^{-0.2081}$$

where Y is still measured in units of £000, and X is in million units. This gives an AVC curve declining somewhat throughout its length. A comparison of AVC values derived from the linear and logarithmic forms, respectively, is shown in the accompanying table.

Output, million units	AVC, pence per unit	
	Linear regression	Log regression
100	0.473	0.543
300	0.380	0.432
500	0.362	0.388
700	0.354	0.362
1,000	0.348	0.336
1,100	0.347	0.329
1,200	0.346	0.323

output is a linear one, both for different firms of varying plant capacity and for a single firm at different levels of plant size.

Finally, in order to estimate the long-run cost function of economic theory, it remains to study the variation of capital charges with output as the firm moves from one plant scale to another. The published British statistics are of no assistance in this matter. An attempt to obtain information from leading manufacturers of generating equipment also proved abortive because of the secrecy surrounding the cost of current projects and the limited number of projects completed in the past by any single firm under conditions of approximately constant factor prices. The only statistical data obtainable on this topic are in the useful "Station Cost Surveys" compiled by the *Electrical World*, and these data relate exclusively to American stations. The largest postwar survey[1] gives the following relevant data for over 100 undertakings in 1947:

1. Installed capacity (in eight grades rising to 200,000 kilowatts plus)
2. Output
3. Annual fixed charges per unit of output

These fixed charges consist of such items as land, structures, boiler plant equipment, turbogenerator unit, accessory electrical equipment, etc., assessed for all the firms in the survey at 15 per cent per annum, and expressed per unit of output. The two serious drawbacks of the data for our purpose are the exclusion of management costs, and the fact that the plant costs depend not only upon the amount of plant but also upon the date at which it was installed. Some of the firms in the survey were still operating plant originally installed in the decade 1910–1919. Roughly speaking, plant and construction costs were fairly high in the twenties, low in the thirties, and high again in the postwar period.[2] Thus the true relationship between fixed charges and installed capacity will be obscured by any differences in the age structure of the equipment of different firms. Furthermore, the relationship between fixed charges and output, which we require, is influenced by variations in load factors between firms. Nevertheless, a sufficiently large number of firms will help to average out these variations and give

---

[1] A. E. Knowlton, "Fifth Steam Station Cost Survey," *Electrical World*, vol. 130, July, 1948, and J. P. Anderson, "Trends in Construction Costs," *Edison Electric Institute Bulletin*, vol. 15, no. 11, November, 1947.

[2] *Ibid.*

some idea of the relationship obtaining between annual fixed costs
and output. Omitting those undertakings using fuels other than
coal (so as to conform to the British firms) left 73 firms. There

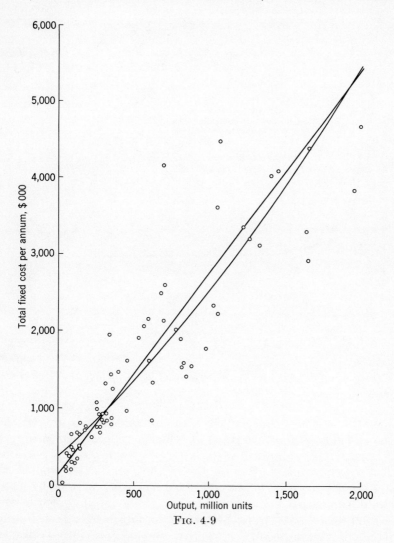

Fɪɢ. 4-9

remained the choice of working with the annual fixed cost data in
total or average form. Both methods were used, and the data are
shown in Figs. 4-9 and 4-10.

As can be seen from Fig. 4-9, where total fixed cost per annum is plotted against output, the majority of the observations are in the lower output ranges so that it is difficult to determine the shape of the relationship over the whole range. A simple linear regression yields the equation

$$Y' = 132.3 + 2.6387X$$

where Y = total fixed costs per annum, $000, and X = output, million units. The corresponding correlation coefficient is 0.9212.

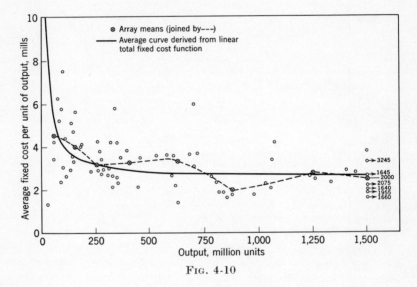

Fig. 4-10

A term in X^2 here proves significant, yielding a curvilinear regression

$$Y' = 382 + 1.8030X + 0.0003674X^2$$

with $R = 0.9301$. Despite the significance test it is difficult to choose between the linear and curvilinear regressions, owing to the unsatisfactory nature of the data. For example, it is possible that the larger plants had proportionately greater extensions of plant in the last decade, when construction costs were high. This would help to account for the curvilinear regression, but it is impossible to check this hypothesis from the data as the age structure of each firm's equipment is not given. Secondly, all capital charges have been computed at an arbitrary 15 per cent. Larger utilities, however, are probably able to borrow at a lower rate than the smaller firms, and this again would tend to straighten out the curvilinear regression.

A supplementary aid in choosing between the two regressions is to consider the average cost data shown in Fig. 4-10. In addition to the original scatter, the array means for various output ranges and the average fixed cost curve derived from the linear total regression are shown. The latter falls very steeply at first and then tends to flatten out into a practically horizontal straight line, and it seems to describe adequately the variation in the data. It is important to note the distinction between this *AFC* curve and the *AFC* curve of short-period analysis. The latter relates to a given level of total fixed cost, which is constant for the range of output studied, yielding in consequence a rectangular hyperbola asymptotic to both axes. The *AFC* curve of this section shows average fixed (capital) costs per unit of ouput as output varies over a wide range of different plant scales, and we conclude that, apart from the steep initial fall, this curve approximates to a horizontal straight line over the major part of the range of possible outputs.[1] The intrafirm and the interfirm studies above also show that the other component of long-run average cost [namely, average working (variable) cost per unit of output] is of approximately the same

[1] In a cross-section study of capital costs a second important explanatory factor in addition to output will be the load factor at which different stations are operated. Fitting a logarithmic function to the United States data for 1947 gives

$$Y' = 8.898X^{0.9476}e^{-0.011,495P}$$

where P = plant factor, per cent (ratio of actual net output to that obtainable over 8,760 hours of full rated capacity operation), $R^2 = 0.9161$, $R = 0.9572$. Holding plant factor constant at its average level of 66 per cent for the 73 firms gives an alternative estimate of *AFC*, which is a closer approximation to a horizontal straight line than the *AFC* curve from the linear regression shown in Fig. 4-10. Comparative values are as follows:

Output, million units	*AFC*, mills per unit	
	Linear form	Log form
50	5.3	3.39
200	3.3	3.16
500	2.9	3.01
750	2.80	2.95
1,000	2.77	2.90
1,250	2.75	2.87
1,500	2.72	2.84

shape—falling steeply at first and then flattening out into a practically horizontal straight line (as a consequence of the total variable cost regression being linear). Therefore the long-run average cost curve will have the same basic shape as its two components—falling steeply at first, and then being approximately constant over the major part of the output range.

Finally, a last way of studying the long-run average cost curve is to compute the parameters of an equation which incorporates

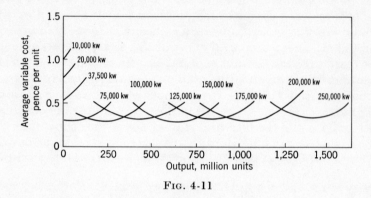

Fig. 4-11

plant size explicitly into the analysis. As data on AC (i.e., $AFC + AVC$) do not exist, the variables with which we work are

Y = average variable cost, pence per unit of output
X = output, million units
Z = plant size, thousands of kilowatts

By least-squares analysis we then obtain the parameters of the following general equation:

$$Y' = a + b_1X + b_2X^2 + cXZ + d_1Z + d_2Z^2$$

This yields the following regression for data relating to 56 sample firms in 1946–1947.

$$Y' = 1.238,950 + 0.003,256X + 0.000,002,926X^2$$
$$- 0.000,046,18XZ - 0.026,081Z$$
$$+ 0.000,183,89Z^2 \quad \text{with } R = 0.5894$$

The next step is to hold plant size constant at the following values (in kilowatts)—10,000, 20,000, 75,000, 100,000, 125,000,

150,000, 175,000, 200,000, and 250,000—and compute the equation of the AVC curve for each case. The results are shown in Fig. 4-11, and they lend strong support to the previous analysis. The minima of successive AVC curves lie on a practically horizontal straight line, substantiating the results of the 23 long-period and 2 cross-section studies given above. (The individual, short-period curves are U-shaped, but this follows automatically from the inclusion of X^2 in the equation and the fact that no significance tests were applied.) As before, the envelope to these curves is only the first component of long-run average cost, but if Fig. 4-10 is a reliable indication of the second (capital cost) component, then long-run average cost is approximately constant over large ranges of output, or, in other words, the economies of scale in electricity generation can be fully exploited by firms of medium size.

CONCLUSIONS

To summarize, our aim has been to derive the net relationships between cost and output in both the short and long period, in order to see to what extent the cost-output relationships of economic theory are substantiated by actual experience in this industry. This has required the removal from the cost data of the influence of factors other than output changes by the use of index numbers of price and quality and the subsequent use of multiple correlation analysis in conjunction with the usual statistical tests of significance in order to "choose" between alternative regressions.

From the short-period data presented in Table 4-6 it is seen that the weight of evidence is in favor of the third type of cost situation outlined in Chap. 2 (see Fig. 2-3). Marginal and average variable costs are constant over the observed range of output, while in electricity generation the capacity of the existing plant sets an absolute limit to the output range. AC at first falls steeply and then flattens out, tending toward the constant MC line as an asymptote.

The estimation of long-run average cost is much more dubious owing to the severe defects of the available data on capital costs. After an initial fall, average working costs are approximately constant over the rest of the output range, and the capital cost data tend to support a similar thesis with respect to AFC. Long-run average cost, therefore, falls quickly and steeply, thereafter approximating to a horizontal straight line.

Section 4-2. Road Passenger Transport

This section presents the results of a statistical investigation of the relationship between output and costs in a single road passenger transport firm over a period of time and of the relationship between scale and costs in a cross section of firms at a given period of time. Time-series data on costs and output are also available for the cross section of firms, so that it is possible to picture graphically a group of short-run curves for firms of different sizes.

The firm for which we have detailed information is one of the larger undertakings in the United Kingdom with an operating staff of about 3,500 and a fleet of over 1,300 vehicles, which supply about 45 million car miles of transport each year. The bulk of the firm's activity consists of the provision of ordinary stage and express services on which about 190 million passenger journeys are made each year; in addition there are some tours and special contract services. These activities bring in a gross revenue of about £3¾ million annually.

For planning and accounting purposes the year is divided into thirteen 4-week periods and most of the important statistics for these periods show a very marked seasonal pattern. Figure 4-12, for example, shows the behavior of three basic statistics over the years 1949 to 1952; the first series, car miles per period, displays a very regular seasonal movement with a maximum in the eighth period and a minimum in the thirteenth period each year. Receipts per car mile show an equally strong seasonal pattern, but the outline is not quite so smooth, and the series also shows an upward trend, as a general increase in fares took effect at the beginning of 1951 and a selective increase in August of that year. Thus not only does the undertaking provide more car miles in the summer but these car miles make a greater average contribution to revenue than do those of the winter months. Total expenses per car mile display a reverse, though weaker, seasonal pattern, the higher degree of utilization of equipment and staff in the summer months leading to a reduction in unit costs. If the graph of receipts per car mile were superimposed on that of expenses, the two would intersect to give a "scissors" effect, showing profits being earned in the summer and losses incurred in the winter. This allocation of the year's total profit between the constituent 4-week periods is arbitrary, in that it depends on the spread of the year's fixed costs over these periods, and it is quite possible that the application of a different principle for spreading the fixed costs could eliminate the losses of the winter, reduce the profits of the summer, and leave the year's net profit unchanged.

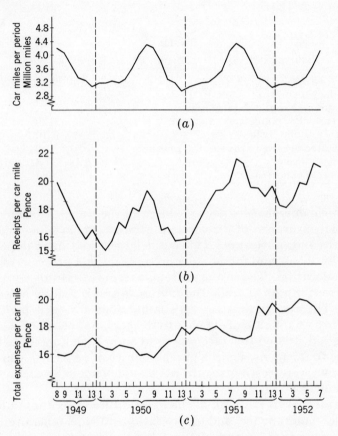

FIG. 4-12. (*a*) Car miles per period; (*b*) receipts per car mile; (*c*) total expenses per car mile.

In the same sense, of course, any given year's profit is arbitrary, depending upon the method employed to assess the cost of the current services of the firm's land, buildings, and equipment. This arbitrary element in costing is unavoidable, and a statistical cost-output relationship only has meaning in relation to the underlying pattern of fixed cost allocation. The importance of this arbitrary element in the present context depends upon the relative size of the expense items affected by it, and so we must look at the composition of the figure for total expenses per period.

Table 4-8 shows the breakdown of the total expenses figure and the relative importance of the various components, based on data for the year 1951.

TABLE 4-8

PERCENTAGE COMPOSITION OF TOTAL EXPENSES, 1951

	Cost category	Percentage of cost
A	Vehicle operating	62
B	Maintenance and depreciation (vehicles, plant, and equipment)	20
C	Other traffic costs	10
D	Maintenance and renewal of structures	2
E	Vehicle licenses	3
F	General expenses	3

Vehicle operating expenses consist of the wages, clothing, and national insurance of drivers and conductors, gasoline and fuel oil, tires and lubricants. This is the largest and most important element of cost and fortunately presents no real problem of arbitrary allocation. The cost of all items except tires is directly related to current inputs of labor and materials and is readily ascertainable. The cost figures for tires is obtained for each period by applying a fixed rate of expense to the period's actual mileage; in the period studied this rate was fixed anew each quarter to allow for the frequent rises in the purchase price of new tires, which by mid-1952 were costing two-thirds as much again as at the commencement of 1949.

In category *B* the bulk of the expenditure is accounted for by vehicle maintenance and depreciation. Vehicle maintenance, which consists of expenditure on labor and materials in about the ratio of two to one, varies fairly directly with car miles; vehicle depreciation is charged on a strict mileage basis, on the assumption of a 12-year life for a bus chassis and a 6-year life for the body. The recorded figures for maintenance of plant and equipment fluctuate from period to period in a rather arbitrary fashion without showing any relationship to car miles. A fixed charge was made each period for plant and equipment depreciation, and it might reasonably be argued that the maintenance and depreciation for plant and equipment should be excluded from the cost figures. We did not trouble to do this as both figures account for only about ½ per cent of total expenditure.

Other traffic costs consist of the wages, etc., of traffic staff, bus cleaning, tickets, miscellaneous expense such as the cost of tolls, and finally compensation and insurance of vehicles. These cost items are in the main directly influenced by the number of car miles run per period, and we include them all in the total expenses figure.

The maintenance and renewal of structures is a cost item which bears no direct relation to current car miles, the figures recorded for each period being the expenses actually incurred in the 4 weeks and not some arbitrary allocation of the year's estimated total expenditure. Vehicle licenses may be taken out for as short a period as a month, and so this cost item is fairly directly related to current output. The final item of general expenses is a grouping of such items as salaries, office expenses, rent, rates, publicity, and insurance. These are approximately constant from period to period and account for about 3 per cent of total expenses.

Cost categories A, B, and C thus account for over 90 per cent of total expenses and are in the main composed of items which are directly related to current output. We accepted, therefore, the total recorded figures of cost in each 4-week period as the basis of our analysis, subject to deflation for factor price changes. For this purpose we constructed separate price indices from the firm's records for wages, fuel, and tires (in category A), for maintenance and depreciation (B),[1] other traffic costs (C), and maintenance and renewal of structures (D). The rate of license duty did not change during the period studied, and the collection of cost items under general expenses (F) was so miscellaneous that, in view of its small percentage share in the total expenses and the more stable behavior of prices in this group, we did not adjust for these price changes.

Figure 4-13a to d illustrates the relation of the more important items of deflated cost to car miles. For both wages and fuel costs the relationship is seen to be strong and linear. The adjustment of

[1] This index was constructed by combining with appropriate weights a price index of the materials used and a wage rate index based on the rates for electricians, engineers, greasers, and body builders. This index applies specifically to maintenance expenditure, which constitutes about two-thirds of expenditure in category B, but it was used to deflate the total expenditure in this group, on the assumption that replacement prices would be fairly closely related to the prices of the materials and labor involved.

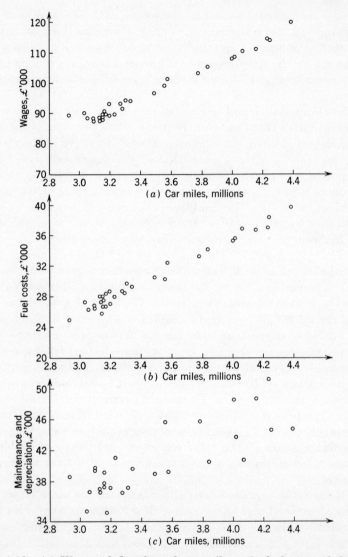

Fig. 4-13. (*a*) Wages (deflated) and car miles; (*b*) fuel costs (deflated) and car miles; (*c*) maintenance and depreciation (deflated) and car miles; (*d*) other traffic costs (deflated) and car miles; (*e*) total expenses (deflated) and car miles.

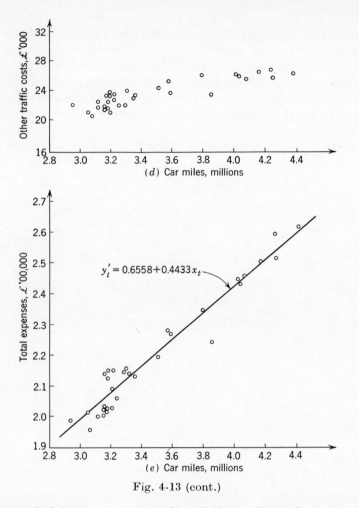

Fig. 4-13 (cont.)

the recorded fuel costs was made as follows. Since fuel costs are,
by definition, equal to total mileage multiplied by the price per
gallon and divided by mileage per gallon (mpg), the correction we
require is given by

$$\text{Corrected fuel cost} = \text{observed fuel costs} \times \frac{\text{mpg}[1]}{\text{price per gal}} \quad (4\text{-}1)$$

That is, we adjust the observed costs not only for price changes,

---

[1] This ratio was expressed in index number form, and its value in the
first period set equal to unity.

but also for changes in the efficiency of utilization of fuel as measured by mileage per gallon. This latter factor would be influenced by changes in the quality of the fuel supplied or by changes in the type of bus, etc. The situation was further complicated by the use of two types of fuel, namely, fuel oil and gasoline, and by a steady shift from the latter to the former throughout the period studied. Thus for the correction defined by (4-1) above, we must use average miles per gallon and average price per gallon, where the averages are taken over both fuels in each 4-week period.

TABLE 4-9
VARIABLES FOR THE TIME-SERIES ANALYSIS

Total deflated expenses y_t and car miles x_t per period

Period	Total deflated expenses, £00,000 y_t	Car miles, millions x_t	Period	Total deflated expenses, £00,000 y_t	Car miles, millions x_t	Period	Total deflated expenses, £00,000 y_t	Car miles millions x_t
−12		3.111	3	£2.153	3.197	18	£2.132	3.338
−11		3.125	4	2.153	3.173	19	2.195	3.492
−10		3.143	5	2.154	3.292	20	2.437	4.019
−9		3.136	6	2.282	3.561	21	2.623	4.394
−8		3.247	7	2.456	4.013	22	2.523	4.251
−7		3.621	8	2.599	4.244	23	2.244	3.844
−6		3.995	9	2.509	4.159	24	2.153	3.276
−5		4.151	10	2.345	3.776	25	2.025	3.184
−4		4.055	11	2.059	3.232	26	2.007	3.037
−3		3.689	12	2.027	3.141	27	2.018	3.142
−2		3.289	13	1.985	2.928	28	2.021	3.159
−1		3.196	14	1.956	3.063	29	2.004	3.139
0		3.061	15	2.004	3.096	30	2.093	3.203
1	£2.139	3.147	16	2.001	3.096	31	2.139	3.307
2	2.126	3.160	17	2.015	3.158	32	2.270	3.585
						33	2.464	4.073

The resultant deflated fuel costs display a strong linear relationship with car miles. As might be expected, the relationship of maintenance and depreciation to car miles is less strong, but there is a suggestion that it is positive and linear. Other traffic costs also increase fairly steadily with output and the over-all result, as shown in Fig. 4-13e, is a fairly strong linear relationship.

We now proceed to estimate the parameters of this cost-output relationship from the data given in Table 4-9. In this transport undertaking car miles was a basic decision variable. Toward the end of each year the car mile budget was laid down for the 13 forthcoming periods, largely by duplicating the marked seasonal pattern of the current year. There existed, however, some flexibility in the adjustment of car miles actually supplied to changing conditions and variations in local needs. Thus the above decision-taking procedure may be described by the relation

$$x_t = \alpha_0 + \alpha_1 x_{t-13} + u_t \tag{4-2}$$

which states that car miles run in period t are equal to a linear function of the car miles run in the corresponding period of the previous year plus a disturbance term u_t. The graph of car miles in the first section of Fig. 4-12 shows that we may expect α_0 to be close to zero and α_1 close to unity.

If y_t represents total deflated costs in period t, then the cost function may be written

$$y_t = \beta_0 + \beta_1 x_t + v_t \tag{4-3}$$

where v_t represents a disturbance term. The procedure followed in the statistical estimation of the βs now depends upon the assumptions made about the disturbances u and v. If one assumes that u_t and v_t follow a joint normal distribution with zero means, unknown but constant variances, and zero covariance and if in addition the u,v values are serially independent, then it would follow that the straightforward application of least squares to y_t and x_t would yield maximum-likelihood estimates of the βs. The application of least-squares methods to (4-2) and (4-3) separately, with 33 pairs of observations in each case, gives

$$x_t = -0.1969 + 1.0643 x_{t-13} + u_t \tag{4-4}$$

$$r = 0.9888$$

$$d = \frac{\Sigma (\Delta u)^2}{\Sigma u^2} = 1.0067$$

and
$$y_t = 0.6497 + 0.4467 x_t + v_t \tag{4-5}$$

$$r = 0.9729$$

$$d = \frac{\Sigma (\Delta v)^2}{\Sigma v^2} = 1.1585$$

The correlation between the u,v residuals is $r_{uv} = 0.1595$, so that the assumption of independence between the two disturbances seems a reasonable one, but the d values, on reference to the significance points tabulated by Durbin and Watson,[1] indicate significant positive serial correlation at the 1 per cent level in each set of residuals. This is a fairly common situation in econometric work and it is customary to attempt to resolve it by taking first differences of the original observations, before carrying out the statistical computations. This is equivalent to assuming that the autoregressive structure of the disturbance term is represented to a sufficient degree of approximation by

$$u_t = u_{t-1} + \epsilon_t \tag{4-6}$$

where ϵ_t is independent over time. For small ϵ this implies a very high positive value for the first autocorrelation of the u's. As an alternative we assumed an autoregressive structure for both the u's and v's of the form

$$u_t = 0.5u_{t-1} + \epsilon_t \tag{4-7}$$

and thus transformed each of the three variables y_t, x_t, and x_{t-13} by means of $(1 - 0.5E^{-1})$, where E^{-1} denotes the preceding value of a variable. Applying least squares to the transformed variables, we obtained the following estimates of the αs and βs:

$$a_0 = 0.2016, a_1 = 1.0650, r = 0.9811, d = 2.0837 \tag{4-8}$$

$$b_0 = 0.6558, b_1 = 0.4433, r = 0.9536, d = 2.7709 \tag{4-9}$$

The correlation coefficient between the residuals in the analysis based on transformed variables is 0.1231. Thus the transformed variables more nearly satisfy the assumptions underlying least-squares statistical procedure. The first value of d gives no indication of serial correlation of the residuals, the second value gives a significant indication of negative serial correlation at the 5 per cent but not at the 1 per cent level, and the correlation between the two sets of residuals is very low.

Comparing Eqs. (4-4) and (4-5) with Eqs. (4-8) and (4-9), it will be seen that the estimates of regression and correlation coefficients come out very close together for the untransformed and transformed data. We take as our estimates of the parameters of the total cost function the results in (4-9), and the resultant straight line is shown in Fig. 4-13e. For values of car miles ranging from 3.2 to 4.0 million, the elasticity of this total cost function ranges

[1] J. Durbin and G. S. Watson, "Testing for Serial Correlation in Least-squares Regression, II," *Biometrika*, vol. 38, parts 1 and 2, 1951, pp. 159–178.

from 0.68 to 0.73, so that we may conclude that an increase of 10 per cent in output is associated on the average with an increase of 7 per cent in total costs. The short-run average cost function is thus downward sloping to the right throughout its length, an increase of 10 per cent in output being associated on the average with a 3 per cent reduction in average costs per unit of output.

An approximate idea of the shape of the long-run cost function is obtained from an examination of cross-section data for a group

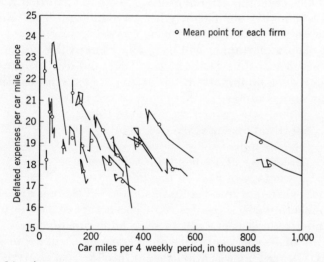

Fig. 4-14. Average cost curves for firms of different sizes. ○ = mean point for each firm.

of different-sized firms at a given period of time. This tends to eliminate the influence of extraneous variables, such as prices, which vary with the passage of time, and if the variations in plant size are sufficiently great we obtain a picture of how cost varies over a wide output range. Data collected by a standard accounting procedure were made available for 24 firms. Figure 4-14 shows the short-run average cost curves for 22 different undertakings in the first seven 4-week periods of 1952. The cost figures shown on the graph here have been deflated for factor price changes and the mean point is also shown for each undertaking. The coordinates of the latter are given by the mean 4-week output and the simple average of the expenses per car mile figure in each of the 7 periods. The points for successive periods are joined together and the general trend of each short-run cost curve is downward sloping to the right, as we have already found for the single undertaking analyzed in detail above. With regard to the long-run relationship between costs and output, there is a fairly substantial dispersion in costs at any given output level, but nevertheless there does appear to be a tendency for costs to fall at first with increases in output and then to stabilize so that for outputs of 200,000 car miles or more no further economies of scale accrue.

We must now see if the cost-output relationship suggested by Fig. 4-14 still remains after account is taken of any other relevant factors which vary significantly between undertakings. For this purpose we use annual data relating to 1951, given in Table 4-10, so that each undertaking will have experienced the full range of the normal seasonal variation in its output, and we further assume that there were no important variations in factor prices between different undertakings.

The variables with which we work are then

$X_1 = $ log (total expenses per car mile)
$X_2 = $ log (car miles)
$X_3 = $ percentage of double deckers in fleet
$X_4 = $ percentage of fleet on fuel oil

Car miles is brought into the analysis to see if there is any significant connection with expenses. The percentage of double deckers in an undertaking's fleet ranged from a minimum of 5 per cent to a maximum of 100 per cent, with an average figure of about 50 per cent, so this variable was also brought into the cost analysis. The percentage of the fleet on fuel oil may also be expected to influence expenses per car mile since all the undertakings in the group showed a higher mileage per gallon of fuel oil than per gallon of gasoline, the over-all averages being 11.8 and 8.8 miles, respectively, and this advantage was not offset by any price differential, for fuel oil was in fact slightly cheaper than gasoline in 1951.

The matrix of zero-order correlation coefficients is

	X_1	X_2	X_3	X_4
X_1	1.0000	−0.4371	0.5774	0.0355
X_2		1.0000	−0.5287	−0.1825
X_3			1.0000	0.5512
X_4				1.0000

As expected, we find a negative correlation between average expenses and car miles and a positive connection between expenses

TABLE 4-10

VARIABLES FOR THE CROSS-SECTION ANALYSIS, 1951

(24 undertakings)

Thousands of car miles in year	Expenses per car mile, pence	Receipts per car mile, pence	Percentage of double deckers in fleet	Percentage of fleet on fuel oil	Car miles per car per week
6,235	19.76	25.10	100.00	100.00	785
46,230	17.85	19.23	43.67	84.53	656
7,360	19.96	21.42	65.51	81.57	578
28,715	16.80	18.11	45.16	93.33	812
21,934	18.20	19.24	49.20	83.07	733
1,337	16.71	19.31	74.84	94.99	688
17,881	18.81	20.07	70.66	92.34	711
2,319	20.74	24.35	63.93	95.08	725
18,040	16.56	17.60	14.45	61.24	642
1,147	18.55	20.13	68.58	97.90	560
2,176	17.40	18.40	53.33	97.50	709
13,267	17.62	18.96	25.16	56.86	514
3,581	21.24	25.75	35.76	63.58	448
15,104	18.23	19.40	47.72	95.29	748
47,009	16.86	18.64	17.21	100.00	841
10,139	17.45	19.10	43.15	89.40	668
6,147	17.66	20.00	67.73	92.54	686
23,089	18.30	19.31	33.27	67.53	598
20,550	16.58	20.49	26.61	98.32	800
9,450	17.51	17.07	61.35	86.72	N.A.
1,028	21.17	20.61	100.00	100.00	N.A.
3,848	16.92	15.73	5.35	65.58	N.A.
15,656	16.96	18.70	20.53	93.72	683
7,725	18.24	18.99	50.59	96.63	703

and percentage of double deckers, but the simple correlation between expenses and percentage of the fleet on fuel oil is very small and has a positive sign rather than the anticipated negative. However, these are only zero-order correlation coefficients, and crucial questions of interpretation arise. For example, we have seen that expenses are negatively related to car miles and positively related to the percentage of double deckers, but car miles are in turn negatively related to the percentage of double deckers, $r_{23} = -0.5287$; that is, the larger undertakings tended in general to have a lower percentage of double deckers in their fleets. Is then the negative relationship between average expenses and car miles due mainly to the direct influence of car miles or to the indirect effect through car miles of the third variable, percentage of double deckers? This type of question is answered by looking at the partial correlation coefficients, which are

$$r_{12.34} = -0.1406$$
$$r_{13.24} = 0.5742$$
$$r_{14.23} = -0.3977$$

Thus the simple correlation between expenses and car miles is reduced by about two-thirds when the influence of the other two determining variables is removed, and the resultant value (-0.1406), while it has a negative sign, is not significantly different from zero at the 5 per cent level. The correlation of expenses with percentage of double deckers, however, remains large and positive in the four variable analyses, and emerges as the strongest influence on unit costs, being significantly different from zero at the 1 per cent level. The effect of the fourth variable, percentage of fleet on fuel oil (-0.3977), also comes out quite strongly in the 4 variable analyses, the negative sign agreeing with theoretical expectation and the coefficient differing significantly from zero at the 5 per cent level (on a one-tail test). Thus the effect of the full analysis is to reduce substantially the apparent connection between long-run costs and output indicated in Fig. 4-14, the size of the partial correlation coefficient being too small in relation to the number of observations on which it is based for us to conclude with any certainty that long-run costs decline with increasing output.[1]

Our conclusions may be summarized as follows:

1. The detailed analysis of a single large undertaking with a substantial seasonal variation in output showed its short-run average cost to be a decreasing function of output over the whole of the observed output range.

2. There was some indication that long-run average costs also decline with output, but it was not strong enough to lead to the rejection of the hypothesis that long-run average costs do not vary with output.

---

[1] "... the omnibus trade conforms perhaps to the law of constant return." A. Marshall, *Principles of Economics*, 8th ed., Macmillan & Co., Ltd., London, 1938, p. 458, footnote 2.

Section 4-3. Multiple-product Food-processing Firm

This section examines the cost-output relationships experienced in a multiple-product firm. The firm selected for study was a medium-sized food-processing firm producing directly for sale to the retail market. The period analyzed was one of just over 9 months from September, 1950, to June, 1951. During this time the firm was producing a "hard core" of about 10 different products continually, while some other products were falling out of production and being replaced by new ones. As many products were perishable (within 2 to 3 days), much of the above production was in direct response to orders from the firm's retail outlets, and as these varied substantially from week to week there was considerable variation in individual output figures. An additional source of such variation was the fact that some raw materials were subject to seasonal changes in supply. The firm also produced certain stand-by products ("fillers") which were storable and whose ingredients were not subject to seasonal variation in supply. The output of these was varied so as to counterbalance the other output variations largely beyond the firm's control and thus maintain a fairly even flow of total activity. In addition to the above there was some production on special contracts, but the latter had to be ignored in our analysis as the "product" was by no means the same from contract to contract.

An elaborate and efficient accounting system produced weekly figures showing, among other things, (1) physical production of each type of product, and (2) total direct costs of each product subdivided according to the four categories of materials, labor, packing, and freight. The over-all weekly allocation of indirect charges consisted of the cost of such items as salaries, indirect labor, factory charges, laboratory expenses, etc. These remained fairly constant over the period studied, and there was no attempt to allocate them between products, although arbitrary accounting rules exist for such allocation.

This accounting data made it possible to analyze the cost-output variations from two different angles. First, it was possible to study the variations of direct cost with output for each product separately, and, secondly, to study the variation of aggregate direct cost with variations in total output. Both analyses require the prior removal from the cost data of the influence of factor price changes, of which there were several in the period studied. It was possible

TABLE 4-11

TABLE 4-11

REGRESSION ANALYSES FOR SEPARATE PRODUCTS

Product (1)	Trans-formation (2)	No. of weeks (3)	$Y =$ (4)	a (5)	bX (6)	r (7)	δ^2/s^2 (8)	CV, per cent (9)
A	1	37	$Y =$	3.5	$+0.1115X$ ± 0.0022	0.9935	1.62	41
B	1	37	$Y =$	-5.9	$+0.1620X$ ± 0.0042	0.9884	1.61	34
C	1	36	$Y =$	181.6	$+4.9293X$ ± 0.2940	0.9445	2.67†	27
	$1 + E^{-1}$	35	$Y =$	238.0	$+5.1455X$ ± 0.1942	0.9773	0.97‡	
	$1 + 0.3141E^{-1}$	35	$Y =$	183.3	$+5.0722X$ ± 0.2327	0.9670	1.79	
D	1	29	$Y =$	4.7	$+0.4165X$ ± 0.0251	0.9544	2.49	57
E	1	24	$Y =$	16.9	$+3.6432X$ ± 0.0454	0.9983	1.66	71
F	1	14	$Y =$	13.8	$+3.4448X$ ± 0.0957	0.9954	1.75	38
G	1	7	$Y =$	72.2	$+4.0384X$ ± 0.5111	0.9622	1.43	31
H	1	18	$Y =$	-31.5	$+5.4472X$ ± 0.1460	0.9943	1.29§	50
	$1 - E^{-1}$	17	$Y =$	-0.7	$+5.1324X$ ± 0.1576	0.9930	2.57	
I	1	14	$Y =$	-90.6	$+5.0368X$ ± 0.2592	0.9845	2.60	21
J	1	20	$Y =$	8.4	$+0.1192X$ ± 0.0051	0.9842	1.71	53
K	1	17	$Y =$	-0.7	$+0.0920X$ ± 0.0019	0.9967	2.15	64
L	1	16	$Y =$	-16.2	$+0.0687X$ ± 0.0045	0.9709	2.36	23
M	1	20	$Y =$	168.1	$+1.5711X$ ± 0.1846	0.8950	1.22§	26
	$1 - 0.3774E^{-1}$	19	$Y =$	73.8	$+1.8734X$ ± 0.1138	0.8709	2.38	
N	1	9	$Y =$	1.2	$+0.1111X$ ± 0.0063	0.9889	2.15	69

Y = total deflated direct cost.
X = output.
† Indicates significant negative serial correlation at the 5 per cent level.
‡ Indicates significant positive serial correlation at the 1 per cent level.
§ Indicates significant positive serial correlation at the 5 per cent level.

to construct from the firm's records a factor price index number for each category of direct costs for each product and these were employed to deflate all four sets of cost figures, yielding a weekly total deflated direct cost figure for each product.

In the statistical analysis which follows we have used the single-equation least-squares approach. For each equation the randomness of the residuals has been tested and an appropriate transformation employed when the original residuals were nonrandom. As we have shown in Chap. 3, single-equation least-squares methods may be applied to the cost function even when the firm is actively adjusting its output level to maximize profits or to maintain a desired level of stocks. In the present case many outputs were outside the *direct* control of the firm. This was the joint result of several factors. Being of medium size in an oligopolistic industry the firm was largely a price follower, so that it exercised little direct control over its price range. Moreover, demand was influenced by other factors, which were to a large extent outside the firm's control (for example, most demands displayed a pronounced seasonal variation). Thus at a given price, weekly sales were found to fluctuate widely. The perishable nature of many products meant that weekly outputs were dictated by the weekly orders received from retail outlets, while on the supply side the perishable nature of many materials meant that they had to be utilized as soon as possible after the crop was picked. For these reasons it is not possible to write down any simple and realistic output-determination equation, and so we have studied the cost function on its own, treating output as an exogenous variable.

Table 4-11 presents the regression analysis for each of the separate products produced during the period studied. The two variables for each product are total deflated direct cost and output, both measured per week. All observations relate to full working weeks so as to avoid the complications due to changes in the length of the work period.

For most products the output observations are scattered over a sufficiently wide range to justify the fitting of regression lines, the average coefficient of variation being 43 per cent, which compares fairly favorably with the averages of 45 per cent and 55 per cent for the two groups of firms in the electricity study.[1]

From an inspection of the correlation coefficients and the illustrations in Fig. 4-15, it is seen that a simple linear regression gives an excellent fit in all cases.

Taking the 5 per cent level as critical for either positive or negative serial correlation of the residuals, it is seen from the values of von Neumann's ratio in column (8) that 11 out of the 14

[1] See Tables 4-3 and 4-4 above.

equations in terms of the original variables give residuals which are satisfactorily random. Of the 3 remaining values, 1 is indicative of negative serial correlation and the other 2 of positive serial correlation. In the case of negative serial correlation the first

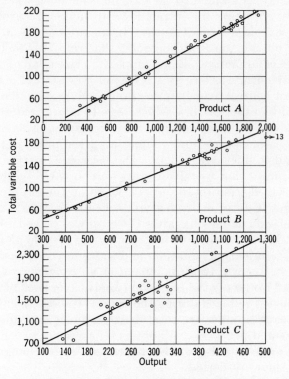

FIG. 4-15. Cost-output relationships.

difference transformation is, of course, inappropriate. Let the regression be of the form

$$Y_t = a + bX_t + u_t \tag{4-10}$$

where Y and X are variables in original units and u is the residual. Suppose

$$u_t = -\beta u_{t-1} + \epsilon_t \tag{4-11}$$

where ϵ is a random residual. Then substituting for u_t in (4-10) we have

$$Y'_t = a' + bX'_t + \epsilon_t \tag{4-12}$$

where the residual is random, and where

$$Y'_t = Y_t + \beta Y_{t-1}$$
$$X'_t = X_t + \beta X_{t-1}$$

(4-13)

If we assume, as a first approximation, that $\beta = 1$, then the appropriate transformation of the variables as indicated by (4-13) is to sum successive pairs of values. This was tried for product C, but the residuals of the transformed relationship were highly positively correlated.

A second approach was therefore tried, in which we attempted to estimate the autoregressive structure of the residuals in the original equation. This was done by computing the residuals Z from the original regression equation and estimating the parameters of the first lag difference equation

$$Z_{t+1} = \alpha - \beta Z_t$$

by least-squares methods. The value found for β was 0.3141, with a correlation coefficient of 0.3173, and a new autoregressive transformation was tried of the form

$$Y'_t = Y_t + 0.3141 Y_{t-1}$$
$$X'_t = X_t + 0.3141 X_{t-1}$$

(4-14)

This produced a regression with random residuals, $\delta^2/s^2 = 1.79$, which is fairly close to the expected value of 2.06 for a random series of this length. It is interesting to note that the correlation coefficient for the transformed series is actually higher than that for the original series, and that the difference between the two regression coefficients $(5.0722 - 4.9293)$ is less than one standard error.

A similar stability of correlation, and to a lesser extent of regression, coefficients is found for the other two transformations (products H and M). In the case of product H, a first difference transformation gives residuals which are satisfactorily random, and no attempt was made to estimate more precisely the autoregressive structure of the residuals. The correlation coefficients are 0.9943 (original) and 0.9930 (transformed), but this time the difference between the regression coefficients is equal to about two standard errors. For product M a first difference transformation produced residuals which were highly negatively correlated. The fitting of a first lag difference equation of the form, $Z_{t+1} = \alpha + \beta Z_t$, to the original residuals gave a value for β of 0.3774, with $r = 0.3954$, and so the autoregressive transformation

$$Y'_t = Y_t - 0.3774 Y_{t-1}$$
$$X'_t = X_t - 0.3774 X_{t-1}$$

(4-15)

was tried. This gave satisfactory residuals, $\delta^2/s^2 = 2.38$, as compared with an expected value of 2.1 for a random series of this length. The correlation coefficient was only slightly reduced, but the regression coefficient was significantly higher.

To summarize, the analysis of the joint variation of direct cost with output for each product considered separately shows that in every case total direct costs may be considered a linear function of output. Marginal cost is therefore constant over the observed range of output. Strictly speaking the average direct (variable) cost curve only coincides with the constant horizontal MC curve if the total direct cost function passes through the origin. Where the intercept on the vertical axis is very small, the AVC curve quickly approaches the MC line asymptotically. Alternatively, the intercept on the y axis, where positive, may be regarded as an element of fixed cost.

Cost Interrelationships

When a firm is producing several different products simultaneously, the question arises whether, and to what extent, the production costs of any particular product may depend not only on the concurrent output of that product but also on the concurrent outputs of all other products.

The existence of such interrelationships may be tested as follows. Let the outputs of the k products at time t be denoted by X_{1t}, X_{2t}, ..., X_{kt}, and the associated total variable costs for each product by Y_{1t}, Y_{2t}, ..., Y_{kt}. Corresponding to each product we may define an output index I_{st} $(s = 1, 2, \ldots, k)$, which measures the output of the other $k - 1$ products at time t. These output indices are of the base-weighted aggregative form with selling prices used as weights.

The test for cost interrelations is then to compute the partial correlation coefficient between Y_s and I_s with X_s held fixed, for each product, and test for significance. A priori we would probably expect $r_{YI.X}$ to have a positive value. For a completely satisfactory test we must investigate for each of the products (1) the randomness, or otherwise, of the residuals from the multiple regression plane, and (2) the confluence problem, since we have now introduced a second explanatory variable.

The results are presented in Table 4-12. Considering the partial

TABLE 4-12

COST INTERRELATIONSHIPS

Product	No. of observations	$r_{YI.X}$	δ^2/s^2	r_{IX}
(1)	(2)	(3)	(4)	(5)
A	37	0.4033†	2.05	−0.5049
B	37	0.5058‡	2.32	−0.1548
C	36	0.1232	2.50	−0.2224
D	29	0.2386	2.70†	−0.2235
E	24	−0.2076	1.98	−0.1350
F	14	−0.6797†	2.82	0.3545
G	7	−0.5641	1.54	−0.5428
H	18	0.5074†	1.84	0.3678
I	14	0.0372	3.24†	0.1014
J	20	−0.1114	1.81	0.2546
K	17	0.3010	2.49	0.0097
L	16	−0.3788	3.11†	−0.3958
M	20	0.4319	1.14†	0.4834
N	9	−0.4337	2.12	−0.5135

† Significant at the 5 per cent level.
‡ Significant at the 1 per cent level.

correlation coefficients shown in column (3), it is seen that 6 of the 14 coefficients have negative signs, contrary to theoretical expectation. Of the 8 positive coefficients, 3 are significantly different from zero. In all, only 4 of the 14 coefficients differ significantly from zero, 3 at the 5 per cent level and 1 at the 1 per cent level. On this test the evidence is, in the main, against the hypothesis of cost interrelations. That is, in 10 of the 14 cases, the statistical explanation of the cost variation is not significantly improved by including an index of the concurrent outputs of the other products as a second explanatory variable. The firm was thus able to vary the outputs of individual products within very wide limits without significantly disturbing the constancy of average variable costs. This was mainly due to the general similarity of the processes used to produce the various products, the adaptability of the labor force, and the flexibility of the equipment. An official of the firm indicated that it was strictly impossible to give a single and valid definition of the firm's capacity; it could only be defined in terms of the relative outputs of particular products or groups of products.

Columns (4) and (5) of Table 4-12 show that the conditions necessary for the application of significance tests to the partial correlation coefficients are in general fairly well satisfied. The residuals from the regression plane are significantly nonrandom in only 4 cases and then only at the 5 per cent level and not at the 1 per cent level. The correlation between the two explanatory variables is generally quite low, being numerically greater than 0.5 in only 3 cases.

VARIATION OF AGGREGATE DIRECT COST WITH AGGREGATE OUTPUT

Aggregation of the direct cost figures presents no difficulty since they are all in money terms. But heterogeneous outputs cannot be simply added together. A suitable method of aggregation may be found by noting that the most important aspect of a product from the firm's point of view is its revenue-producing capacity. When one product is substituted for another, the main consideration is the change in net revenue. Therefore we constructed an index of aggregate output by weighting the quantities by the initial selling prices of the various products, and summing over the products produced in each period. This latter series and the aggregate direct cost figures were both expressed in index number form, so as not to reveal any confidential information, and the relationship between the two examined.

The coefficient of variation for the output index was 28 per cent so that there is a reasonable spread of observations. A simple linear regression of cost on output yields the following result,

$$Y = 6.1981 + 0.9875X$$

with $r = 0.9783$. This regression is shown in Fig. 4-16. The residuals, however, indicated significant positive serial correlation at the 1 per cent level. The rough estimation of the autoregressive structure of the residuals from the original equation suggested the following transformation $(1 - 0.4707E^{-1})$. The resultant regression equation was

$$Y' = 3.2 + 0.9913X'$$

with $r = 0.9686$ and $\delta^2/s^2 = 2.48$ ($N = 36$), which falls short of the 5 per cent level of significance for negative serial correlation. As can be seen, the correlation coefficient in each case is very high, and the estimates of the regression slope very close together. The standard error of the estimate of the regression slope, calculated from the transformed data, is 0.0436, and the difference between the two estimates is much less than this.

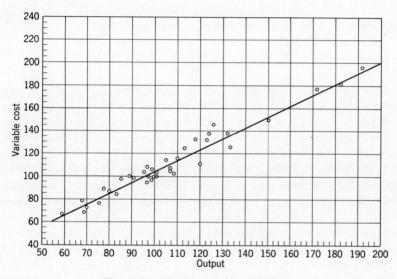

FIG. 4-16. Output and cost indices.

Since the intercept on the cost axis is very small, the approximate elasticity of the relationship between the cost and output indices is unity—a given percentage change in aggregate output (as measured by the index) tending to produce an almost equal percentage change in total direct costs. This also implies an equal percentage relationship between gross profits and output. It is, however, unlikely that in fact gross profits could be indefinitely extended *pari passu* with output, for, while the regression function is a fairly good fit to the observed data, its prolonged extension in either direction is inadmissible. An extension upward involves the implicit assumption that substantially higher levels of output can still be sold at the previous prices, since the fixed weights in the output index are product selling prices. This is unlikely to be true, and any attempt to sell greatly increased quantities at the same prices would probably lead to disproportionate increases in selling costs. If neither of these limits operates quickly, existing productive capacity would soon set a limit to aggregate output.

Another possible approach to the construction of the output index is to use average variable costs as weights. The resultant index makes possible a joint test of the constancy and independence of the average variable costs of the separate products. Let b_i $(i = 1, 2, \ldots, k)$ indicate the average variable cost for each product, as measured by the regression equations of Table 4-11. Then the output index for period t becomes

$$I_t = \sum_{i=1}^{k} b_{it} X_{it}$$

This is, in fact, an estimate of what aggregate variable cost would be if average variable cost were constant for each product and independent of the outputs of the other products. Correlating the actual aggregate variable cost with this index should then give a correlation coefficient and a regression slope which both approach $+1$ the more perfectly the two assumptions are realized. The appropriate analysis gives $r = 0.9699$ and $b = 0.9407$. The standard error of b is 0.0399, so that the regression slope does not differ significantly from unity. Although the variable cost weights are not proportional to the price weights, owing to the variations in gross profit margins, the results of the two analyses are not dissimilar.

The statistical finding of constant and independent average variable costs for each product lends considerable indirect support to the basic hypotheses of the linear programming school, in so far as it is desired to apply those techniques to the theory of the firm.[1] Their definition of a productive "process" is equivalent to that of a linear homogeneous production function with the supplementary condition that the inputs can only be varied en bloc by equal proportionate amounts. If we regard each product as being produced by a separate "process," then each has a linear total variable cost function and this linearity also obtains for each category of variable cost (though the detailed evidence for this would take up too much space to include here). With constant factor prices linearity of cost functions implies linear, homogeneous production functions.

However, our analysis relates only to the variable factors, and

[1] See R. Dorfman, *Application of Linear Programming to the Theory of the Firm*, University of California Press, Berkeley, Calif., 1951.

the core of the linear programming theory centers around the input matrix, which specifies the quantities of the fixed or limited factors required in order that each process be carried on at unit level.[1] The nature of these limited factors makes it very difficult to obtain similar statistical evidence for them, since these are the items (land, buildings, machinery, tools, etc.) which are usually lumped under Factory or General Overhead and seldom allocated to specific units of output. Possible indicators such as floor space occupied, machine hours, etc., might reasonably be expected to behave in a similar fashion to the variable inputs, but it seems doubtful if one of the limiting factors, namely, entrepreneurial time and ability, has necessarily to be stepped up pro rata with increases in the level of a process. In general it would seem difficult to measure the intensity of use of most fixed factors by different processes at unit level, so as to provide the basic information required for the input matrix. On the other hand, some limited factors may not be fixed capital goods. In times of very full employment a firm may be unable to expand its labor force; under various forms of planning and control a firm may be allocated a specific amount of some scarce raw material or producer good—tinplate, steel, sugar, etc. These all become limited factors in the meaning of the linear programming analysis, which is then directly applicable.

Section 4-4. Costs in Coal Mining

This section contains an examination of the variation in production costs in the 70 collieries which comprise the North Western Division of the National Coal Board. The results are in striking contrast to those reported elsewhere in this book, for no firm relationship is found between average costs and size of colliery.

The tremendous variability in natural conditions, methods of working, and financial results in the British coal mining industry is notorious. As the Royal Commission on the Mining Industry (1925) reported,[2]

> The only generalization about it that is safe is that no generalization is possible. The industry cannot therefore be regarded as a collection of more or less uniform undertakings, employing so many men under conditions fairly similar, producing a single article, the costs of production and the price obtained varying little among them at any time.

[1] *Ibid.*, pp. 23–25 and 67–69.
[2] *Command Paper* (Cmd) 2600, pp. 44–45.

Average costs will reflect the total impact of all the diverse factors which vary from pit to pit. But we may roughly classify these factors into three more or less distinct groups, namely, geological, technical and mechanical, and human.

GEOLOGICAL FACTORS

The main geological factors have been well summarized by the Royal Commission:[1]

> The depth of the coal seams from the surface: the thickness of the seams: the chemical composition of the coal: the degree of its mixture with dirt or with other impurities: the soundness or unsoundness of the roof and floor in the workings of the mine: the quantity of water to be dealt with in sinking the shafts and in working the seams: the degree of danger from gas: the presence of faults in the seams and their inclination: the gradients at which the roadways have to be made through the coal.

These factors vary substantially from coal field to coal field and also from pit to pit within a coal field, and constitute the unalterable legacy of nature to which the mining engineer must adapt himself as best he can by devising the most appropriate types of equipment and methods of working. Equal inputs of labor, power, equipment, supplies, and managerial ability will therefore produce unequal results in terms of output and average costs owing to the unequal geological handicaps that have to be overcome.

The geological factors, combined with the age of the mines and extensive working in the past, are particularly disadvantageous in the North Western Division.[2]

> When the coal seams that underlie Lancashire were formed Nature was in her most unpredictable mood: in almost any mine in the country you can see a good five-foot seam vanish into barren rock through geological faulting .... To go down a pit is to see economics in the raw. The first thing that knocks the platitudes out of you is the walk to the coal face. The tunnel rises and falls with the seam, so that at one moment you are climbing a sort of black Pennine scree and at the next landing heavily on the battery of your safety lamp as the gradient gets the better of your legs. And all the time you are larding the lean earth like a Falstaff as the air becomes progressively hotter .... The uncertainty of nature is

---

[1] *Ibid.*, p. 44.

[2] "The Fight for Coal in Lancashire," *Manchester Guardian*, March 11, 1953.

such that again and again profit turns to loss in a few yards. Faulting has meant that Lancashire mine workings have penetrated to the greatest depths in Gt. Britain—in one pit to 4,072 feet.

ECHNICAL AND MECHANICAL FACTORS

As well as an inheritance from nature of deep and twisted seams and varying strata conditions, the present management of the industry has also to cope with the legacy of previous managements as reflected in the layout of the mines, both above and below ground, the degree of exhaustion of the reserves and the age of the mine, especially as reflected in the distance of the faces from the shaft, the type and condition of the electrical and mechanical equipment, and the often awkward sizes of the mines produced by the initial distribution of the ownership of the mineral. All these factors seriously delimit and circumscribe the actions that can currently be taken to influence productivity. Once again, equal labor and nonlabor inputs applied now may yield very unequal results because of the differing technical environments in which they have to be applied. In some cases the reserves may be so close to exhaustion that technically feasible improvements would not repay their initial cost. In many other cases the initial layout and method of working may be completely unsuited to the adoption of the most efficient and modern mechanical methods. This is particularly true with regard to the introduction of the horizon system of mining and the securing of the associated economies in the system of haulage, and a period from 2 to 10 years is thus required for the radical reconstruction of an existing colliery.

The National Coal Board, in line with the recommendations of the Technical Advisory Committee on Coal Mining,[1] has pushed ahead with attempts to mechanize as many operations as practicable. The basic stages in the mining of coal are (1) cutting, (2) loading, (3) conveying, and (4) washing and grading. At a given pit the degree of mechanization may be different at each stage, and pits may differ from one to another in the degree of mechanization at all stages. Stage 2 in 1950 was hardly mechanized in the North Western Division and only a minute fraction of the 1950 output was power-loaded. Three variables, however, indicate the extent of mechanization at stages 1, 3, and 4. These are:

Percentage of Coal Machine Got. This excludes tonnage got by mechanical picks alone, but includes coal got by mechanical picks

[1] *Command Paper* (Cmd) **6610**, 1945.

with coal cutters, coal got by coal cutters alone, and coal got with cutter loaders.

Percentage of Coal Conveyed. This relates to the method of moving coal from the face. The percentage indicates the amount loaded on to conveyors, as distinct from tubs. Practically all this loading is done by hand, only 4 pits in the division having some power loading in 1950.

Percentage of Cleaned Coal Mechanically Cleaned. Salable output consists of (1) mechanically cleaned, plus (2) hand cleaned, plus (3) untreated coal. This figure is $a/(a + b)$, expressed as a percentage.

TABLE 4-13

EXTENT OF MECHANIZATION IN 62 COLLIERIES OF
NORTH WESTERN DIVISION, 1950

Per cent	Number of collieries		
	Stage 1, cutting	Stage 3, conveying	Stage 4, washing and grading
100	35	26	2
90–99	13	17	2
80–89	4	8	5
70–79	4	2	8
60–69	3	1	12
50–59		1	8
40–49			2
30–39			1
20–29		1	
10–19	1	1	2
1–9			6
0	2	5	14

Table 4-13 indicates the extent of mechanization at each stage in the 62 pits in 1950. We see that half the pits had 100 per cent mechanization of the cutting stage and another fifth had more than 90 per cent but less than the full 100 per cent mechanization of this stage. The extent of mechanization of conveying (stage 3) was very similar to that at stage 1, and it is only at the cleaning stage that these collieries display a wide spread of mechanization percentages.

Human Factors

A vitally important influence on productivity and costs in mining is the complex of human factors: the relations between management and men, the quality of the planning and supervisory work, the willingness and adaptability of the men, the energy and drive with which they tackle their work, and the amount of voluntary absenteeism, which, being unpredictable, irregular, and often

TABLE 4-14

Output of Salable Coal and Costs per Ton, 1950

Output, thousand tons / Costs per ton, shillings	Under 50	50–100	100–150	150–200	200–300	300–400	400–500	500 and over	Total
65–70				1					1
60–65				1	1				2
55–60		3	2	3	4	1			13
50–55	1		3	2	2	2	3	2	15
45–50	3	3	2	4	2	5	1	1	21
40–45	1	2	1		1			1	6
35–40				1					1
30–35		2					1		3
Total	5	10	8	12	10	8	5	4	62
Average costs per ton	47.5	46.5	51.2	52.9	53.5	50.0	47.5	48.7	50.2

unduly concentrated at certain times, has a disproportionate effect on output in the cyclical system of mining required on longwall faces. Apart from the general state of industrial relations in the industry, this is a factor which can vary from pit to pit. A simple correlation of percentage absenteeism at the coal face with the logarithm of output per man shift gives a negative coefficient of -0.2209 for 62 collieries, and a correlation of the first variable with the logarithm of costs per ton gives a positive coefficient of 0.4109.

This catalogue of factors suggests that we may expect a wide dispersion of costs per ton among the various collieries. Omitting any colliery which either commenced production or closed down during 1950 left 70 pits in full-time production during the year.

Of these 8 were drift mines, in which conditions are not really comparable with the other pits since the coal is extracted directly from the hillside and no shafts have to be sunk, and they have been excluded from the analysis. Table 4-14 shows the distribution of the remaining 62 collieries according to the output of salable coal during the year and the associated production costs per ton. This table reveals the wide variability in costs per ton of salable output. In fact, the highest recorded figure of 69.24 shillings is more than double the lowest of 33.82 shillings. Figure 4-17 shows costs

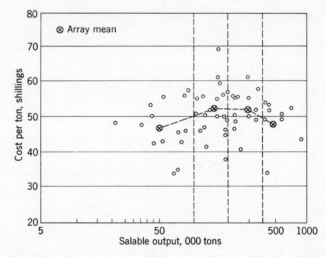

FIG. 4-17. Costs per ton and output for 62 collieries, 1950.

per ton plotted against output for the 62 collieries. There is no evidence here of any real relationship between unit costs and size of output. The array means, shown in the bottom row of Table 4-14 and joined on Fig. 4-17 by a broken line, show that the smallest collieries had as low costs on the average as the largest. Collieries in the 100,000- to 300,000-ton class display higher average (unit) costs, but in view of the small number of observations too much significance should not be attached to this fact. The value of the correlation ratio for the data of Table 4-14 is 0.3767, which may be shown by the usual analysis of variance to be not significantly different from zero. The computed value of F is 1.28 with $n_1 = 7$ and $n_2 = 54$; this falls well short of the F value at the 5 per cent level of significance.

Section 4-5. Building Societies

In this section we examine the operational costs of building societies. These are the full costs of conducting the business of the society, and some information about them is available in the Reports of the Registrar of Friendly Societies. The Registrar classifies societies into groups A, B, and C according as their assets exceed £5 million, lie between £1 and £5 million, or are less than

TABLE 4-15

RATIO OF MANAGEMENT EXPENSES TO £100 OF
MEAN TOTAL ASSETS

Year	Group A		Group B		Group C	
	Shillings	Pence	Shillings	Pence	Shillings	Pence
1952	12	9	10	3	13	2
1951	12	10	10	9	13	3
1950	13	1	10	9	13	4
1949	13	7	11	0	13	10
1948	13	6	12	2	13	11
1947	13	4	11	6	13	7
1946	12	9	10	5	12	8
1938	11	4	9	8	12	3

£1 million, and for each group he publishes the ratio of management expenses to £100 of mean total assets. Table 4-15 shows these ratios for 1938 and 1946 to 1952.

Here at last, it would appear, we have some indication of a U-shaped long-run cost function. The medium-sized societies show a consistently lower ratio than the smaller and larger societies, whose ratios are roughly comparable.

To carry the analysis further, we obtained the 1953 financial accounts of 217 societies with gross income exceeding £4,000. For each society we computed a cost ratio, namely, management expenses expressed as a percentage of the society's gross income. The societies were divided into 6 groups by value of gross income and the mean of the cost ratios was computed for each group. The results are shown in Table 4-16. A U-shaped pattern again appears. There is, however, a considerable spread of the cost ratios within any given size group and so the question arises whether the variation between the mean cost ratios is significant in relation to the variation about the mean values within each size group.

Performing an analysis of variance, we obtain a variance ratio of 4.3, with degrees of freedom $n_1 = 5$ and $n_2 = 207$, a value which

TABLE 4-16

MEAN COST RATIO FOR VARIOUS SIZES OF BUILDING SOCIETY, 1953

Gross income of society, thousand pounds	Number of societies	Mean cost ratio, per cent
£ 4 and under £ 10	30	15.2
10 and under 40	45	12.8
40 and under 100	53	12.0
100 and under 250	42	11.7
250 and under 650	23	12.0
650 and over	24	12.5

TABLE 4-17

MEAN COST RATIOS IN NONBRANCH AND BRANCH BUILDING SOCIETIES, 1953

Gross income of society, thousand pounds	Nonbranch societies		Branch societies	
	No. of societies	Mean cost ratio, per cent	No. of societies	Mean cost ratio, per cent
£ 4 and under £10	27	15.1	4	16.5
10 and under 40	41	13.3	4	14.5
40 and under 100	44	12.0	9	12.8
100 and under 250	30	11.0	13	13.1
250 and under 650	3	10.8	18	12.9
650 and over	4	8.9	20	13.2

is significant at the 1 per cent level; therefore, we conclude that costs are significantly related to size.

There are two distinct types of building society, namely, one which operates without branches and one which does have a branch organization. Two questions then arise. Does the U-shaped pattern hold for each type of society separately, and do the two types of society differ with respect to their average cost level? We therefore subdivide the 217 societies into the two classes of nonbranch and branch societies, respectively, and examine the behavior of the mean cost ratios with increasing size in each class. Retaining the same 6 size groups as in Table 4-16, we obtain the mean cost ratios shown in Table 4-17.

The nonbranch societies are concentrated in the 4 lower size groups of the scale and the branch societies in the top 4. Applying variance analysis to each class separately, the variance ratio for the nonbranch societies is 4.6, which is significant at the 1 per cent level, while that for the branch societies is approximately unity, which does not indicate a significant variation in the mean levels. Thus the U-shaped pattern of the mean cost ratios in Table 4-16 is the net resultant of two separate underlying patterns, namely (1) a cost ratio declining with size in the nonbranch societies and (2) a more or less constant cost ratio in the 4 major size groups in the branch societies. It appears that in comparable size groups the nonbranch societies have a slightly lower cost ratio than the branch societies.

An important assumption underlying the analysis of variance tests is that the variance within each group is approximately constant. It is clear from inspection of the data that this assumption is probably not fulfilled by these data, since the vertical spread of the cost ratios is much greater in the smaller-sized societies than in the larger. The application of Bartlett's test for the homogeneity of a set of variances confirms this suspicion. It is essential, therefore, to examine whether our conclusions about the variation of the cost ratios with size still hold when correction is made for this factor. The appropriate correction is to transform the original data in an attempt to stabilize the variances. It appears from an examination of the data that the standard deviation of the cost ratios within each size group is roughly proportional to the square of the mean cost ratio for the size group. Hence an appropriate transformation is to take the reciprocals of the original observations. Applying variance analysis to the transformed observations in the two classes of nonbranch and branch societies, we find that our original conclusions still hold good, though the level of significance is lower. The variance ratio for the nonbranch societies is now significant at the 5 per cent level and that for the branch societies is still approximately unity and hence nonsignificant. The reciprocal transformation achieved its objective, as the variances of the transformed data did not differ significantly in either class.

Section 4-6. Life Assurance Companies

This section is similar to the preceding one on building societies in that we can again examine costs for a large cross section of companies of widely different sizes to see whether any relationship exists between the size of an organization and the level of its costs.

The following analysis is confined to ordinary life business, where costs consist of all management expenses and commission,

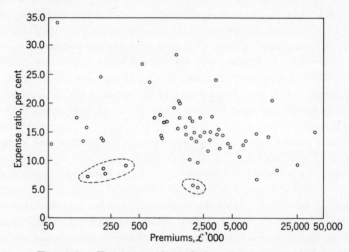

Fig. 4-18.   Expense ratio and size of company, 1952.

the sum of which is expressed as a percentage of premium income to give an expense ratio. We take this ratio as defined and calculated in the Stone and Cox Insurance Tables.[1] The Stone and Cox expense ratio is calculated in such a way as to make a reasonably fair comparison between companies which transact varying amounts of single-premium business.

In Fig. 4-18 we show the expense ratio plotted against premium income for 1952. There appears to be a negative relation between the two, the expense ratio declining, on the average, with increasing premium income. Six companies, enclosed with a broken line,

[1] "In calculating the expense ratio we have deducted the single premiums from the total premium income of the year, and 5 per cent of the amount of the single premiums from the total amount of commission and expenses shown in the reports." Stone and Cox Insurance Tables (Ordinary Branch), Stone and Cox, Ltd., London, 1953, p. 6.

appear on the graph with very low expense ratios; they pay no commission. The correlation coefficient between expense ratio and the logarithm of total annual premiums is -0.3072 which, for 61 observations, is significantly different from zero at the 5 per cent level. A similar calculation for 1938 yields a correlation coefficient of -0.3930.

Classifying the 1952 results into three groups on the basis of the premium income, we obtain the results shown in Table 4-18. The data of Table 4-18 and a "significant" correlation coefficient do

TABLE 4-18

EXPENSE RATIO AND SIZE OF COMPANY, 1952

Total annual premiums, thousand pounds	Number of companies	Average expense ratio, per cent
£ 50 and under £ 500	9	19.3
500 and under 5,000	41	15.9
5,000 and over	9	12.0
All companies	59	15.81

not prove the existence of lower costs as a consequence of larger size. There are two important and relevant factors which require examination. First, an important influence on costs in any year is the *amount of new business done in that year* due to the payment of the initial commission and the other expenses connected with the issuing of the policy. This factor can be allowed for by working out for each company the premium income from new business as a percentage of total premium income and bringing this additional variable into the correlation analysis. Secondly, most of the "schemes" business,[1] which has developed to such an extent in recent years, is done at very low expense rates compared with individual policy business. Thus it is possible that large companies may have a low over-all expense ratio merely because of a large amount of schemes business. A factor, however, which suggests that this is not the whole explanation for low expense ratios in the larger companies is the significant negative correlation for 1938, a year when schemes business had not developed to anything like its postwar importance. A possible method of dealing with this second factor is to divide the companies into fairly homogeneous groups and to carry out the analysis separately for each group. We

[1] Schemes business consists of group life, group endowments with or without pension options, group pensions, etc.

have taken the grouping given in *The Policy Holder* of composite offices, industrial-ordinary offices, and specialist life offices; for each group the three variables analyzed are

X_1 = expense ratio, per cent

X_2 = new premiums as a percentage of total premiums

X_3 = log of total premiums

The results of the analysis are given in Table 4-19. We can leave out of account the 7 industrial-ordinary companies in Table 4-19; The number is very small and all the correlation coefficients

TABLE 4-19

EXPENSE RATIO AND SIZE OF COMPANY, 1952
(Three groups)

Correlation coefficients	25 composite companies	7 industrial-ordinary companies	16 specialist life companies
r_{12}	0.2184	−0.1035	0.5617†
r_{13}	−0.5534‡	0.0674	−0.6192‡
r_{23}	−0.2945	−0.3068	−0.1843
$r_{12.3}$	0.0696	−0.0872	0.5800
$r_{13.2}$	−0.5245‡	0.0376	−0.6342‡

† Significant at the 5 per cent level.
‡ Significant at the 1 per cent level.

are insignificant. For both the composite and the specialist life companies we see that there is a positive correlation r_{12} between the expense ratio and the proportion of new business to total business, which agrees with expectation; there is a strong negative correlation r_{13} between expense ratio and size of company; and there is a suggestion r_{23} that, on the whole, new business is a somewhat smaller proportion of total business in the large companies than in the small. The crucial question is then whether the negative correlation r_{13} between expense ratio and size is evidence of real economies of scale, or whether it is simply due to the smaller relative amount of expensive new business in the larger companies. The answer is given in terms of the partial correlations $r_{13.2}$, which show the net relation between expenses and size when the effects of the varying amount of new business have been eliminated. Both of these coefficients are large and negative, −0.5245 for the composite companies and −0.6342 for the specialist life offices, which suggests the existence of real economies of scale in both groups.

An even better grouping of companies than that provided in Table 4-19 would be one which classified companies solely according to their degree of participation in schemes business. We were fortunate in obtaining a classification of 35 major companies into those

1. Transacting no schemes business
2. Transacting some schemes business
3. Specializing in schemes business[1]

For each of these groups a similar analysis was carried out to the one reported in Table 4-19 above. The results are given in Table 4-20.

TABLE 4-20

EXPENSE RATIO AND SIZE OF COMPANY, 1952
(Companies grouped according to their degree
of participation in schemes business)

Correlation coefficients	13 companies with no schemes business	11 companies with some schemes business	11 specialists in schemes business
r_{12}	0.3157	0.2708	0.2661
r_{13}	−0.4680	−0.3622	−0.7518‡
r_{23}	0.1622	0.2176	−0.6435†
$r_{12.3}$	0.4491	0.3843	−0.4313
$r_{13.2}$	−0.5546†	−0.4482	−0.7868‡

† Significant at the 5 per cent level.
‡ Significant at the 1 per cent level.

The same general pattern emerges in each of the three groups. Expense ratio tends to fall with size (r_{13} negative) and to rise with the proportion of new business to total business. When we consider the net relation between expenses and size, with the proportion of new business held constant, all three partial correlation coefficients are negative ($r_{13.2}$), the levels of significance being 5 per cent, 10 per cent, and 1 per cent, respectively, and in each case the partial coefficient has a greater numerical value than the simple coefficient r_{13}. These results support those found in Table 4-19 and suggest that, when full allowance has been made for other relevant factors, there still remains a significant relation between size and expenses, the expense ratio declining on the average with increasing size of company.

[1] We acknowledge our indebtedness to the editor of *The Policy Holder* and his contributor Lifeman for this classification.

Section 4.7. Labor Productivity and Size of Establishment

The problem considered in this section came to light in the course of an examination of what information, if any, on cost-output relationships might be contained in published census of production reports. We include our analysis of the problem here for two reasons. First, the relationship of labor productivity to size is an important determinant of the cost function, though, unfortunately, even precise knowledge of this relationship does not enable us to say very much about the shape of the cost function. The strongest assertion that can be made is a somewhat negative one. For example, if the ratio of capital to labor inputs increases with the size of establishment, then capital costs per unit of output will probably increase with size; total costs per unit of output can therefore only fall with size if labor costs decline with size and decline sufficiently to offset the rise in capital costs; this latter condition requires labor productivity to increase with size of establishment. If no such increase is found, then total costs per unit of output cannot fall with increasing size (unless we have the unlikely case of a *fall* in the ratio of capital to labor inputs with increasing size sufficient to offset the rising labor costs). On the other hand a rising labor productivity pattern does not guarantee falling average production costs; it is a necessary but not a sufficient condition for that result. A second reason is that the problem considered is a general statistical pitfall, which is an ever-present danger in interpreting grouped data, such as are found in census reports, and our results are relevant to all analyses of this type and thus are not specific to the analysis of labor productivity.

This section examines the relationship between labor productivity and size of establishment in the light of the summary data contained in the Censuses of Manufactures of the United States. In particular, it explores the statistical paradox of the conflicting results that emerge according to the classification methods adopted: the cause of this paradox is explained and suggestions made for establishing correct inferences about the variations of labor productivity with size of establishment.

I

It is a widely held belief that labor productivity tends in general to increase with increases in the size of establishment; and this generalization seems to be strongly supported by the summary tables of the Censuses of Manufactures of the United States. Taking as indicators of labor productivity, value of product per wage earner and also value added per wage earner, we have the results given in Table 4-21.[1] With only two exceptions, both indicators in Table 4-21 record a steady rise in labor productivity with size of establishment in all 4 years.

TABLE 4-21

LABOR PRODUCTIVITY AND SIZE OF ESTABLISHMENT
IN THE UNITED STATES, 1914–1939†

Value of product, thousands of dollars	1914		1919		1929		1939	
	(a)‡	(b)	(a)	(b)	(a)	(b)	(a)	(b)
Less than $5	$1,800	$1,171	$3,647	$2,328				
$ 5–	2,111	1,183	3,787	2,162	$3,801	$2,361	$3,591	$2,088
20–	2,551	1,239	4,501	2,203	4,739	2,800	4,135	2,290
50–					5,542	3,180	4,649	2,454
100–	2,919	1,295	5,213	2,414	5,865	3,101	5,103	2,520
250–					6,102	3,086	5,513	2,583
500–			5,802	2,586	6,504	3,157	5,886	2,713
1,000–					7,088	3,356	6,354	2,923
2,500–	4,763	1,653	8,178	3,017	7,802	3,671	7,652	3,496
$5,000 and over					11,790	4,577	11,247	4,180
All establishments	$3,446	$1,404	$6,862	$2,752	$7,969	$3,607	$7,208	$3,130

† The establishments are classified according to the total value of their product, and the figures cover the establishments in all the trades included in each census.

‡ (a) value of product per wage earner; (b) value added per wage earner.

SOURCES: The figures are computed from the *Fourteenth Census of the United States*, vol. VIII, table 21; *Fifteenth Census of the United States*, Manufactures, vol. I, table 2; and 1939 *Census of Manufactures*, vol. I, chap. 4, table 6.

In 1939, the census establishments were also classified according to the number of wage earners, and in 1947 the only basis of classification employed was number of employees. The results for these two years are given in Table 4-22. These results provide a striking contrast to those of Table 4-21. For 1939 both indicators decline sharply through the first six size classes to a value about 65 per cent of the initial maximum value and thereafter increase, except for product per wage earner which falls again in the final size group. For 1947 the pattern is similar, but less violent: the initial fall only

[1] Our primary concern is not with the relative merits of particular indicators of labor productivity, but rather with the conflicting results that can emerge from census material for any given indicator.

covers three size groups and is only about 20 per cent of the commencing figure: thereafter a rise takes place and then a flattening out and decline at the top end of the size scale. Thus two markedly different patterns emerge for the relationship of labor productivity to size of establishment, depending upon whether the establishments are classified by value of product or number of wage earners.

TABLE 4-22

LABOR PRODUCTIVITY AND SIZE OF ESTABLISHMENT
IN THE UNITED STATES, 1939 AND 1947

No. of wage earners per establishment	1939		1947	
	Product per wage earner, dollars	Value added per wage earner, dollars	No. of employees	Value added per employee, dollars
1–5	$10,074	$4,371	1–4	$5,624
6–20	7,552	3,362	5–9	4,655
			10–19	4,628
21–50	6,772	3,027	20–49	4,864
51–100	6,482	2,940	50–99	5,070
101–250	6,437	2,902	100–249	5,293
251–500	6,421	2,838	250–499	5,416
501–1,000	7,220	3,044	500–999	5,418
1,001–2,500	8,456	3,340	1,000–2,499	5,414
2,501 and over	7,918	3,374	2,500 and over	5,051
All establishments	$ 7,208	$3,130	All establishments	$5,207

SOURCES: U.S. *Census of Manufactures*, 1939, vol. I, chap. 4, table 1; U.S. *Census of Manufactures*, 1947, vol. I, Chap. 3, table 1.

This problem is examined briefly in Steindl's *Maturity and Stagnation in American Capitalism*, but, although his results are mathematically correct, they are economically unenlightening and lead him to accept the classification by value of product, which, as we shall see below, may be a rather dangerous procedure.[1]

[1] J. Steindl, *Maturity and Stagnation in American Capitalism*, Basil Blackwell and Mott, Ltd., Oxford, 1952. Steindl's approach is to pose the question: given a *positive* correlation between the log of value of product per wage earner and log of value of product per establishment, under what conditions is it possible to have a *negative* correlation between log of value of product per wage earner and log of number of wage earners per establishment? Letting r_1 denote the first correlation and b_1 the slope of the linear regression of log of value of product per wage earner on log of value of product per establishment, the answer is that the negative correlation is possible if

$$r_1{}^2 < b_1 \tag{1}$$

The algebra is impeccable, but the following points should be noted.

II

Columns (2), (3), (6), and (7) of Table 4-23 show that value of product and number of wage earners per establishment both increase steadily up the size groups on each basis of classification, but product per wage earner shows two markedly different patterns. This suggests that the cause of the paradox must be related to the two different bases of classification.

Suppose that we have a scatter diagram on which value of product P is measured on the horizontal scale and number of wage earners W on the vertical, each point on the scatter relating to a single establishment, and suppose further that the range of each variable is marked off in certain intervals as in Fig. 4-19.

Classifying the establishments according to value of product or number of wage earners means splitting the diagram into vertical

---

1. The problem which Steindl set himself is not, in fact, the problem raised by the 1939 census results. The latter give a smooth upward movement for labor productivity on the one classification and a down-up-down movement on the other; the condition for this result may possibly be less severe than that required to give a *negative linear* regression in the second case. The completely contradictory patterns do, however, appear for some of the industry groups in Subsection III on page 123.

2. Condition (1) may be written:

$$b_1 b_2 < b_1 \tag{2}$$

where b_2 is the slope of the linear regression of log of value of product per establishment on log of value of product per wage earner. Canceling out b_1, which is positive by assumption, leaves

$$b_2 < 1 \tag{3}$$

Denoting value of product by P and number of wage earners by W, the appropriate regression may be written

$$\log P = a_2 + b_2 \log \frac{P}{W} \tag{4}$$

If we have a series of establishments whose P,W coordinates satisfy (4) exactly, then it follows that for these establishments an increase of x per cent, say, in P/W is associated with an increase of less than x per cent in P. This can only come about if P and W are *inversely* related, if, in other words, the capital structure of these establishments is such that those which are larger as measured by value of product are smaller when measured by number of wage earners. This seems a strange result, and suggests that the regression relationship (4) may sometimes be rather meaningless. It is, therefore, essential to examine the shape of the scatter about this regression in specific cases, and this is done in the Appendix of this chapter.

or horizontal slices, respectively, and then computing for the
establishments in each slice the appropriate statistic such as value
of product per wage earner, or value added per wage earner. If

TABLE 4-23

COMPARISON OF THE TWO BASES OF CLASSIFICATION, 1939

	Classification by value of product				Classification by number of wage earners			
Value of product, thousands of dollars	Value of product per establishment, dollars	Wage earners per establishment	Value of product per wage earner, dollars	No. of wage earners per establishment	Value of product per establishment, dollars	Wage earners per establishment	Value of product per wage earner, dollars
(1)	(2)	(3)	(4)	(5)	(6)	(7)	(8)
$ 5–	$ 11,235	3.13	$3,591	1–5	$ 26,939	2.67	$10,074
20–	32,167	7.78	4,135	6–20	83,615	11.07	7,552
50–	71,066	15.29	4,649	21–50	219,042	32.34	6,772
100–	158,628	31.08	5,103	51–100	461,855	71.25	6,482
250–	354,120	64.23	5,513	101–250	1,002,245	155.70	6,437
500–	701,923	119.25	5,886	251–500	2,230,629	347.38	6,421
1,000–	1,524,304	240.35	6,354	501–1,000	4,946,892	685.15	7,220
2,500–	3,437,122	449.17	7,652	1,001–2,500	12,499,101	1,478.13	8,456
5,000 and over	15,017,720	1,335.25	11,247	2,501 and over	37,094,179	4,684.84	7,918

SOURCE: U.S. *Census of Manufactures*, 1939, vol. I, chap. 4, tables 1 and 6.

there are n establishments in a given group, then for that group

$$\text{Value of product per establishment} = \frac{\Sigma P}{n}$$

$$\text{Number of wage earners per establishment} = \frac{\Sigma W}{n}$$

$$\text{Value of product per worker} = \frac{\Sigma P}{\Sigma W} = \frac{\Sigma P/n}{\Sigma W/n}$$

Thus geometrically the value of product per wage earner for the
establishments in a group is given by cot ϕ, where ϕ is the angle
formed by the P axis and the straight line joining the origin to the
point whose coordinates are $(\Sigma P/n, \Sigma W/n)$. If product per
worker is to *increase* from one group to another, then the angle ϕ
must *decrease* from the first group to the second (and vice versa).
This relationship is illustrated in Fig. 4-20. M_1, M_2, and M_3 are
three group means which indicate rising labor productivity, since
the angle made with the P axis decreases as we move from group
1 to 3.

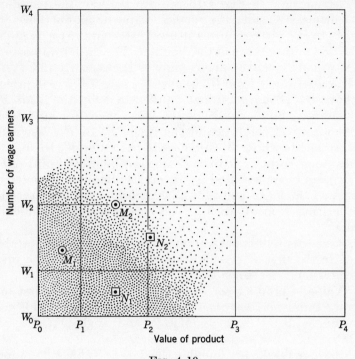

Fig. 4-19

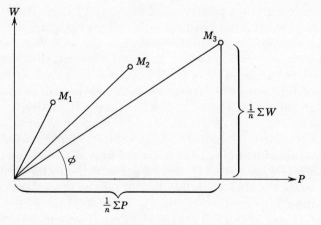

Fig. 4-20

Referring now to Fig. 4-19, we can see how the paradoxical effect arises. Consider the smallest value of product size group from P_0 to P_1: this comprises all establishments, say n' in number, in the first vertical slice of the diagram. For these establishments $\Sigma P/n'$ will obviously be about midway between P_0 and P_1. But the W values range from W_0 to over W_2 and $\Sigma W/n'$ will probably lie above W_1. These coordinates suffice to define the point M_1 on the diagram. Similarly M_2 is the mean point for all establishments whose P value lies in the range P_1 to P_2. For the n'' establishments whose W value lies in the range W_0 to W_1, the P values range from P_0 to over P_2 and so the mean point ($\Sigma P/n''$, $\Sigma W/n''$) can be represented by N_1 on the diagram. Similarly N_2 represents the mean point for all establishments in the second W classification, from W_1 to W_2. This type of pattern produces two results:

1. Value of product per worker is much smaller for the establishments in the first P classification than for those in the first W classification, since angle $M_1OP >$ angle N_1OP.

2. Value of product per worker increases from the first to the second P group and decreases from the first to the second W group, since angle $M_1OP >$ angle M_2OP, and angle $N_1OP <$ angle N_2OP.

Both these results are found in the data in Table 4-23; product per wage earner in the first P classification is $3,591 compared with $10,074 in the first W classification, and movement to the second classification gives a positive and negative change, respectively.

We have postulated nothing so far about the general shape of the W,P scatter other than the condition, shown in Fig. 4-19, that it is so wide, in relation to the W,P grid adopted, that the points at the lower end lie in more than a single cell. This is an essential condition for the initial divergence between the values of product per wage earner on the two classifications. It is also a realistic assumption, because of the tremendous numerical predominance of small-sized establishments. For example, 43 per cent of all the census establishments in 1939 fell in the first W size group (that is, had 5 or less wage earners), and 33 per cent fell in the first P size group, while the corresponding figures for the second size groups are 28 and 23 per cent, respectively. Even if all the 33 per cent in the first P size group fell also in the first W size group, which is extremely unlikely, there would still be 10 per cent of all the establishments with W values between W_0 and W_1 but with P

values greater than P_1, so that the condition on the scatter is satisfied. A similar condition at the top end of the scatter, with not all the points being contained in the top right-hand cell, would suffice to open up an opposite divergence between the W and P means and possibly produce a fall in labor productivity in the last W size group, an effect which is sometimes found in the census data.

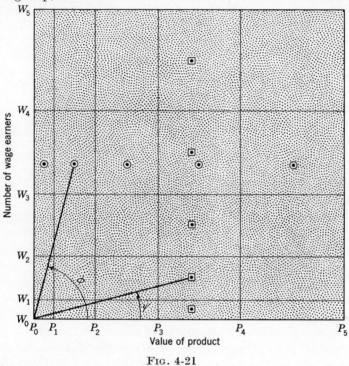

FIG. 4-21

The various patterns that may emerge for labor productivity according to the classification employed on a given set of census data may now be outlined. The distinction between the various cases rests on the initial assumptions which we make about the nature of the W,P scatter.

CASE A: ZERO CORRELATION IN THE W,P SCATTER

We assume here that the points of the scatter are fairly evenly spread over the W,P grid. If ⊙ denotes the mean points $\Sigma P/n$, $\Sigma W/n$ for the P size groups and ⊡ denotes the mean points for the W size groups, then the results will be as shown in Fig. 4-21.

The P classification gives value of product per wage earner $=$ cot ϕ, which *increases* steadily as P increases; and the W classification gives value of product per wage earner $=$ cot ψ, which *decreases* steadily as W increases. Thus, starting with a case in which there is no connection at all between W and P, one emerges with apparently emphatic indications of a strong relationship, positive or negative, between labor productivity and size, depending upon the method of classification employed.

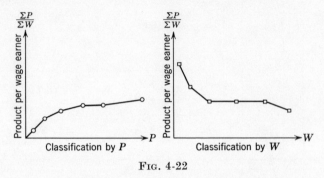

Fig. 4-22

CASE B: POSITIVE CORRELATION IN THE W,P SCATTER

The most probable W,P pattern is perhaps one in which the points slope roughly up the diagram from left to right; it is necessary to distinguish three subcases, according to whether there is a tendency toward constant, increasing, or decreasing labor productivity.

1. *Constant Labor Productivity.* If there is a tendency toward constant labor productivity, the points on the W,P scatter will be distributed approximately around a straight line through the origin, the slope of the line, referred to the W axis, indicating the average productivity level. Owing to the effect described above, the pattern that will emerge for labor productivity will probably be as indicated in Fig. 4-22.

In general, the P classification will show labor productivity rising at first, then tending to stabilize around a constant level in the middle size groups and possibly tending to rise again in the highest size groups; the pattern for labor productivity from the W classification will be the reverse of this. If the W,P scatter is sufficiently wide, the tendency toward constant labor productivity in the middle-sized groups on each classification will disappear, and this case merges into case A with completely conflicting indications as to labor productivity from the two classifications. The condition for the two classifications to give steadily increasing and steadily decreasing productivity figures is that the lines from the origin to the P means should describe successively smaller angles and those to the W means successively larger angles, as indicated in Fig. 4-23. In the case of approximately linear regressions, this merely requires that the intercepts made by the regressions on the appropriate axes should be positive. It is obvious

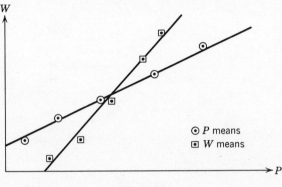

FIG. 4-23

from the diagram that this may occur even when the regression lines are very close together, the correlation between W and P fairly high, and the scatter correspondingly narrow. Using small letters to denote deviations from the means, the condition on positive intercepts may be written

$$\frac{\Sigma wp}{\Sigma p^2} < \frac{\overline{W}}{\overline{P}} \quad \text{and} \quad \frac{\Sigma w^2}{\Sigma wp} > \frac{\overline{W}}{\overline{P}}$$

and hence

$$r_{wp} < \frac{v_p}{v_w} \quad \text{and} \quad r_{wp} < \frac{v_w}{v_p}$$

where r_{wp} is the correlation between W and P, and v denotes the coefficient of variation (the ratio of the standard deviation of a variable to its mean). In the case where the two coefficients of variation are fairly close together, the smaller of the two ratios will still be close to unity so that the W,P scatter can be fairly narrow and still give rise to the contrary indications on labor productivity.

2. *Increasing Labor Productivity.* It is difficult to define unambiguously what sort of pattern on the W,P scatter will correspond to a case of increasing productivity. But there are two main
considerations: first, points displaying increasing productivity

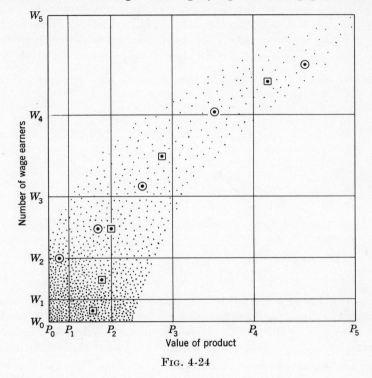

Fig. 4-24

with size will slope up the W,P diagram in such a way as to describe successively smaller angles with the horizontal axis at the
origin; and secondly, there will almost always be observations
fairly close to the origin in the smallest W and P size groups.
Hence we may say that a case of increasing productivity will tend
to give a W,P scatter which is curvilinear and concave from below,
as shown in Fig. 4-24. This would give the labor productivity
patterns shown in Fig. 4-25.

The scatter effect already described would be sufficient to give
declining labor productivity here over the first three W groups.
If there were more than 5 size groups the range of increasing
labor productivity on the W classification would be extended,
and there exists also the possibility of a fall in the final size group.

It is also clear from Fig. 4-24 that if we took a number of heterogeneous industries, most of which showed increasing labor productivity but whose products differed substantially in monetary
value, and if we combined these data on a single W,P diagram,

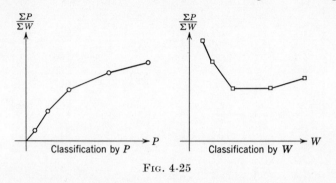

Fig. 4-25

then the scatter would approximate that pictured in case A above,
so that the W classification could show strong signs of decreasing
labor productivity over the whole size range, in spite of the
separate underlying tendencies toward increasing productivity.

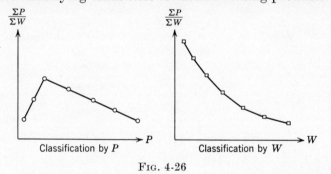

Fig. 4-26

3. *Decreasing Labor Productivity.* This tendency would be described by a curvilinear scatter, convex from below. In this case
the P classification would give a productivity curve increasing at
first and then declining, while the W classification would give a
productivity curve tending to decline through all size groups as
shown in Fig. 4-26.

Case C: Negative Correlation in the W,P Scatter

This is an unrealistic case, included only for the sake of com-
pleteness. If the W,P scatter has a negative slope, it is easy to see

TABLE 4-24
VALUE OF PRODUCT PER WAGE EARNER IN THE UNITED STATES, 1939
(Classification by value of product in thousands of dollars)

Industry group	Size groups (value of product)								
	A $5–	B $20–	C $50–	D $100–	E $250–	F $500–	G $1,000–	H $2,500–	I $5,000 and over
1	$5,679	$7,461	$ 8,855	$ 9,371	$10,161	$11,297	$13,017	$14,853	$22,776
2	2,409	2,192	2,454	2,812	3,527	2,799	3,502	5,626	27,199
3	1,826	2,371	2,728	2,965	3,194	3,364	3,663	4,010	4,320
4	1,878	2,159	2,765	3,955	5,049	5,819	5,515	6,199	7,486
5	1,577	2,289	2,897	3,110	3,280	3,509	3,846	3,957	†
6	3,331	3,787	3,934	3,977	4,137	4,669	4,830	4,314	6,467
7	3,100	3,425	4,053	4,740	5,928	7,203	8,222	9,017	9,720
8	4,685	5,424	5,885	6,566	7,281	7,400	8,875	9,386	18,778
9	7,398	9,657	10,475	11,246	12,109	13,552	14,712	14,070	12,952
10	5,748	7,785	10,780	12,893	15,920	21,000	22,552	23,370	31,351
11	3,659	4,625	5,213	4,799	4,407	4,926	4,473	6,014	10,340
12	3,131	3,494	3,433	3,640	3,594	3,912	4,304	5,362	5,513
13	3,186	3,644	3,750	4,121	4,065	4,719	6,135	5,498	6,713
14	3,720	4,158	4,283	4,669	4,877	5,062	5,840	7,741	8,431
15	4,564	4,826	5,414	5,805	6,375	7,243	8,138	8,942	17,966
16	4,384	5,269	5,243	5,387	5,660	5,806	6,282	6,501	7,930
17	3,918	4,590	5,110	5,463	5,917	6,383	6,274	6,766	6,570
18	4,008	4,501	4,816	5,214	6,086	6,359	6,394	6,710	10,886
19	3,102	3,272	3,187	3,735	4,029	4,451	5,087	5,249	6,389
20	3,446	3,753	4,005	4,047	4,192	4,754	5,090	7,398	12,339
All industry groups	$3,591	$4,135	$ 4,649	$ 5,103	$ 5,513	$ 5,886	$ 6,354	$ 7,652	$11,247

† Indicates that the figure for this cell has been merged with that for the previous cell to avoid disclosure of information relating to one or two establishments.
SOURCE: U.S. *Census of Manufactures*, 1939, vol. I, chap. 4, table 7.

TABLE 4-25
VALUE OF PRODUCT PER WAGE EARNER IN THE UNITED STATES, 1939
(Classification by number of wage earners)

Industry group	Size groups (no. of wage earners)								
	1 1–5	2 6–20	3 21–50	4 51–100	5 101–250	6 251–500	7 501–1,000	8 1,001–2,500	9 2,501 and over
1	$12,716	$11,937	$12,230	$12,316	$11,246	$12,003	$15,052	$20,437	†
2	5,089	2,293	3,993	2,877	11,688	3,278	3,266	23,769	†
3	9,752	4,724	4,325	4,161	3,821	3,556	3,393	3,229	$ 3,642
4	17,443	7,323	4,304	3,694	3,481	3,199	3,478	4,190	†
5	4,345	2,825	3,135	3,037	3,071	3,132	3,057	3,532	
6	6,595	5,028	4,615	4,526	3,949	3,725	3,966	†	
7	8,138	5,841	6,456	7,206	7,905	8,138	8,088	7,197	
8	5,770	5,625	6,120	6,493	7,154	8,121	8,513	13,848	†
9	17,388	15,781	14,016	13,881	14,421	14,040	13,873	9,452	7,312
10	21,673	35,576	32,191	24,865	25,717	24,860	30,819	30,962	27,783
11	9,601	7,894	6,229	5,934	5,563	5,804	6,539	9,184	9,697
12	8,216	5,136	4,838	4,427	4,266	4,219	3,846	3,378	†
13	6,660	5,545	4,374	4,589	5,159	4,458	4,831	5,993	†
14	6,805	6,188	5,865	6,202	6,665	6,697	6,880	6,809	7,578
15	8,979	8,651	6,759	7,892	12,801	11,824	13,794	12,665	†
16	8,384	7,041	7,115	6,823	6,816	6,901	6,590	6,598	6,614
17	6,554	6,065	6,296	6,584	6,405	6,554	6,163	5,779	5,787
18	6,968	6,074	6,717	5,691	7,160	12,244	14,955	9,454	9,752
19	4,607	4,031	4,522	4,528	4,938	5,322	6,245	5,788	5,867
20	5,877	4,933	4,554	4,477	4,262	5,391	5,432	†	†
All industry groups	$10,074	$ 7,552	$ 6,772	$ 6,482	$ 6,437	$ 6,421	$ 7,220	$ 8,456	$ 7,918

† Indicates that the figure for this cell has been merged with that for the previous cell to avoid disclosure of information relating to one or two establishments.
SOURCE: U.S. *Census of Manufactures*, 1939, vol. I, chap. 4, table 3.

that labor productivity will increase steadily with size on the product classification and decrease steadily on the number of wage earners classification. This case is of no practical importance and it would not give, for example, the result noted in Table 4-23 of $\Sigma P/n$ and $\Sigma W/n$ being positively related in all the size groups of either classification.

Of the five cases outlined above, three tend to produce a steadily rising labor productivity curve on the P classification, and the other two will almost certainly give at least an initial rise. It seems clear, therefore, that inferences about the relationship of labor productivity to size can only be established by joint consideration of both patterns. Figures 4-22, 4-25, and 4-26 are probably the crucial patterns and enable us to distinguish between cases of constant, increasing, or decreasing labor productivity. If we find instead that the curve on the P classification slopes steadily upward throughout its length, while that on the W classification slopes steadily downward, then we have an example of case A, where the W,P scatter must be very wide and no relationship can be established. This case would result from the merger of data on insufficiently homogeneous industries, or it may merely reflect a great dispersion of productivity within an industry.

III

To test the validity of the above hypotheses and also to see if apparently conflicting patterns still emerge for finer subgroupings of industry, we present in Tables 4-24 and 4-25 the value of product per wage earner computed from 20 major industry groupings on each basis of classification for the 1939 Census of Manufactures of the United States. The industry groups are:

1. Food and kindred products
2. Tobacco manufactures
3. Textile-mill products and other fiber manufactures
4. Apparel and other finished products made from fabric and similar materials
5. Lumber and timber basic products
6. Furniture and finished lumber products
7. Paper and allied products
8. Printing, publishing, and allied industries
9. Chemicals and allied products
10. Products of petroleum and coal

11. Rubber products
12. Leather and leather products
13. Stone, clay, and glass products
14. Iron and steel and their products except machinery
15. Nonferrous metals and their products
16. Electrical machinery
17. Machinery (except electrical)
18. Automobiles and automobile equipment
19. Transportation equipment except automobiles
20. Miscellaneous industries

These results are summarized in Table 4-26 by counting the

TABLE 4-26

COMPARISON OF THE RESULTS FOR VALUE OF PRODUCT PER WAGE
EARNER GIVEN BY THE TWO BASES OF CLASSIFICATION

No. of increases per industry group	Frequency (number of groups)	
	P classification	*W* classification
8	9	
7	5	
6	5	2
5	1	3
4		7
3		2
2		2
1		3
0		1
Total	20	20

number of increases between successive size groups within each industry for each classification and arranging the results in the form of a frequency distribution. As was to be expected, the *P* classification gives a strong indication of increasing labor productivity in all cases, with 142 increases and only 17 decreases recorded in all the 20 industry groups.[1] The *W* classification gives only 68 increases in all and 79 decreases, and three-quarters of the

[1] The number of decreases between successive size groups for any given industry group will normally be 8 minus the number of increases, since there are only 9 size groups in all. But in some cases, where no figure is shown in the top one or two size groups, the total numbers of differences will be 7 or 6, instead of 8.

industry groups show 4 or less increases per industry group. Comparing the patterns for each industry group in the light of the classifications adopted in Subsection II above, we have the results given in Table 4-27.

Nine industries fit fairly clearly into the increasing productivity pattern. Industries 2 and 10, tobacco manufactures and products of petroleum and coal, do not fit any of our classifications and

TABLE 4-27

LABOR PRODUCTIVITY PATTERNS FOR 20 INDUSTRY GROUPS
BASED ON VALUE OF PRODUCT PER WAGE EARNER

	Pattern	Industry group
B (1)	Constant productivity	5, 16, 17
B (2)	Increasing productivity	1, 7, 8, 11, 13, 14, 15, 18, 19
B (3)	Decreasing productivity	
A	No relationship	3, 4, 6, 9, 12, 20

further subdivision into more homogeneous groups would be desirable in these cases. Figure 4-27 displays some examples of each of the three patterns. Lack of space prevented the correct spacing of the size groups on the horizontal axes, but an attempt has been made to space them in very rough proportion to the actual values, so as not to distort too violently the true shape of each pattern.

It would seem that if only a single basis of classification is possible it is preferable to classify by number of wage earners. This classification alone enables one to distinguish fairly well between cases of constant and increasing productivity; the main difficulty arises where the general tendency of the productivity curve is downward, as this corresponds to both cases A and B (3), and only reference to the productivity curve of the P classification can satisfactorily distinguish between the two. It seems probable, however, that most of such cases will belong to the category of no relationship rather than that of decreasing productivity.

The theory of Subsection II applies directly to the interpretation of the patterns of value of product per wage earner. It is of interest, however, to examine briefly the results which appear for two other commonly used indicators of labor productivity, namely, value added per wage earner, and wages as a percentage of value added. The detailed figures are given in Tables 4-28 to 4-31, and Table 4-32 provides a comparison of the results by showing the

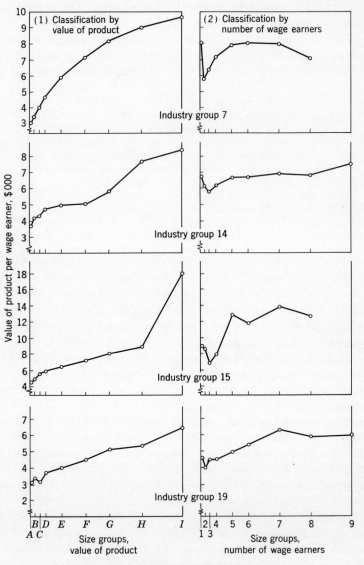

Fig. 4-27. Labor productivity patterns.

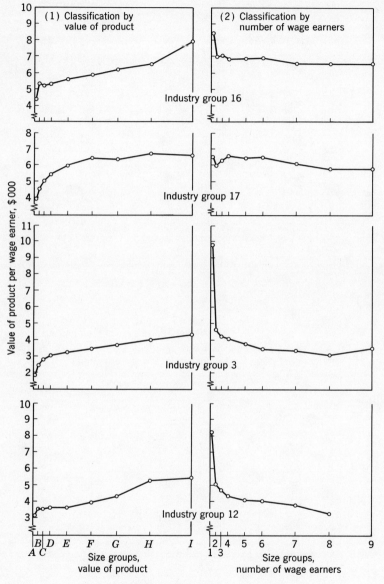

Fig. 4-27 (cont.)

TABLE 4-28

VALUE ADDED PER WAGE EARNER IN THE UNITED STATES, 1939
(Classification by value of product in thousands of dollars)

Industry group	Size groups (value of product)								
	A $5–	B $20–	C $50–	D $100–	E $250–	F $500–	G $1,000–	H $2,500–	I $5,000 and over
1	$2,590	$3,157	$3,526	$3,567	$3,666	$4,025	$4,751	$5,385	$ 5,664
2	1,253	1,110	1,195	1,346	1,601	1,402	1,692	2,441	6,411
3	1,211	1,398	1,444	1,464	1 526	1 533	1,597	1,826	2,159
4	1,278	1,399	1,563	1,770	1,953	2,027	1,965	2,457	2,962
5	957	1,305	1,545	1,599	1,701	1,884	2,134	2,667	†
6	1,793	1,991	2,043	2,000	2,031	2,191	2,389	2,189	3,201
7	1,830	1,886	2,145	2,355	2,656	3,115	3,350	3,807	4,273
8	3,290	3,790	4,119	4,588	5,054	5,114	6,005	6,400	12,377
9	3,567	4,653	5,057	4,970	5,078	5,897	6,475	7,339	7,578
10	2,711	3,086	4,611	4,524	4,424	5,856	5,649	5,817	6,841
11	2,134	2,547	2,774	2,577	2,380	2,576	2,398	2,799	4,293
12	1,682	1,747	1,669	1,632	1,594	1,681	1,806	2,011	2,291
13	2,018	2,276	2,317	2,505	2,535	2,936	3,912	3,742	4,332
14	2,299	2,503	2,484	2,605	2,648	2,738	3,025	3,458	3,247
15	2,854	2,835	2,927	2,922	2,994	3,192	3,451	3,576	4,238
16	2,363	2,810	2,873	2,761	2,825	3,102	3,330	3,845	4,874
17	2,681	3,059	3,221	3,363	3,523	3,837	3,831	4,291	3,812
18	2,193	2,432	2,550	2,674	2,710	3,120	3,081	2,997	3,384
19	1,959	2,035	1,963	2,239	2,287	2,615	2,588	2,936	3,337
20	2,252	2,340	2,408	2,335	2,399	2,656	3,039	5,032	5,082
All industry groups	$2,088	$2,290	$2,454	$2,520	$2,583	$2,713	$2,923	$3,496	$ 4,180

† Indicates that the figure for this cell has been merged with that for the previous cell to avoid disclosure of information relating to one or two establishments.
SOURCE: U.S. *Census of Manufactures*, 1939, vol. I, chapter 4, table 7.

TABLE 4-29

VALUE ADDED PER WAGE EARNER IN THE UNITED STATES, 1939
(Classification by number of wage earners)

Industry group	Size groups (no. of wage earners)								
	1 1–5	2 6–20	3 21–50	4 51–100	5 101–250	6 251–500	7 501– 1,000	8 1,001– 2,500	9 2,501 and over
1	$4,674	$4,244	$4,138	$4,497	$4,111	$4,093	$4,741	$4,135	†
2	2,094	1,242	1,678	1,461	3,762	1,634	1,702	5,616	†
3	3,374	2,142	1,919	1,862	1,723	1,607	1,595	1,505	$2,074
4	5,088	2,621	1,910	1,686	1,514	1,434	1,619	2,211	†
5	2,251	1,467	1,601	1,586	1,638	1,855	1,968	2,426	
6	3,095	2,431	2,176	2,133	2,025	1,907	2,144	†	
7	3,810	2,830	2,891	3,046	3,397	3,377	3,613	3,125	
8	4,044	4,015	4,403	4,656	5,021	5,534	5,807	8,963	†
9	8,256	7,188	6,021	5,757	6,571	7,425	8,714	5,330	5,009
10	7,660	8,138	7,691	5,714	5,626	5,380	6,526	7,981	6,524
11	4,722	4,152	3,121	2,761	2,812	2,896	3,038	3,691	4,245
12	3,276	2,154	1,903	1,872	1,760	1,747	1,674	1,743	†
13	3,702	3,063	2,617	2,838	3,377	2,911	3,157	3,993	†
14	3,681	3,204	2,985	2,978	3,123	2,953	2,998	2,938	3,215
15	3,989	3,382	3,200	3,311	3,672	3,547	4,101	3,655	†
16	4,228	3,631	3,524	3,548	3,548	3,985	3,752	4,063	4,140
17	4,091	3,714	3,785	3,896	3,839	3,980	3,828	3,446	3,538
18	3,449	3,036	3,121	2,745	3,292	3,825	4,105	3,180	3,185
19	2,750	2,315	2,502	2,551	2,587	2,737	2,869	3,060	3,365
20	3,539	2,856	2,515	2,527	2,592	3,149	3,688	†	†
All industry groups	$4,371	$3,362	$3,027	$2,940	$2,902	$2,838	$3,044	$3,340	$3,374

† Indicates that the figure for this cell has been merged with that for the previous cell to avoid disclosure of information relating to one or two establishments.
SOURCE: U.S. *Census of Manufactures*, 1939, vol. I, chap. 4, table 3.

TABLE 4-30

WAGES AS A PERCENTAGE OF VALUE ADDED
IN THE UNITED STATES, 1939
(Classification by value of product, in thousands of dollars)

Industry group	Size groups (value of product)								
	A $5–	B $20–	C $50–	D $100–	E $250–	F $500–	G $1,000–	H $2,500–	I $5,000 and over
1	32.4	29.3	25.9	25.7	26.8	27.3	25.0	23.2	24.7
2	45.4	51.7	51.3	47.5	38.5	43.5	42.3	30.1	14.0
3	54.2	51.0	51.9	52.3	51.4	51.8	52.8	48.2	43.4
4	52.9	59.0	57.3	50.1	44.8	41.5	42.0	45.3	44.5
5	52.3	48.9	46.0	47.1	48.9	52.9	52.8	52.0	†
6	42.1	43.7	42.9	45.0	44.9	42.0	43.5	51.3	43.7
7	38.4	42.6	39.1	38.4	38.5	36.4	36.6	34.0	31.7
8	31.6	32.8	33.6	32.6	30.8	30.9	26.5	27.9	16.2
9	21.5	18.6	18.2	18.7	18.6	18.7	19.2	18.4	19.3
10	30.9	30.5	22.8	23.3	27.9	22.0	25.0	26.2	25.9
11	36.9	33.1	30.9	34.4	38.9	39.5	45.4	42.0	38.1
12	42.7	44.8	48.2	50.6	52.2	50.3	49.9	52.3	46.7
13	40.2	39.9	41.3	41.3	42.7	39.0	32.5	34.6	30.4
14	41.1	41.4	43.0	43.3	43.4	43.8	42.5	39.7	47.4
15	38.6	41.3	40.5	39.4	39.1	37.7	37.1	37.7	33.8
16	38.2	34.6	33.3	36.0	35.8	34.7	35.8	36.1	30.1
17	41.5	40.9	40.1	38.9	36.7	36.1	37.8	34.9	40.0
18	46.5	46.0	45.6	42.3	42.6	38.6	43.0	48.9	49.6
19	49.6	55.5	59.7	57.9	56.5	53.8	55.2	49.3	49.0
20	40.0	40.4	40.8	41.0	41.4	39.2	37.9	29.6	22.7
All industry groups	38.0	39.7	39.0	38.5	38.2	37.9	37.7	34.9	35.4

† Indicates that the figure for this cell has been merged with that for the previous cell to avoid disclosure of information relating to one or two establishments.
SOURCE: U.S. *Census of Manufactures*, 1939, vol. I, chap. 4, table 7.

TABLE 4-31

WAGES AS A PERCENTAGE OF VALUE ADDED IN THE
UNITED STATES, 1939
(Classification by number of wage earners)

Industry group	Size groups (no. of wage earners)								
	1 1–5	2 6–20	3 21–50	4 51–100	5 101–250	6 251–500	7 501– 1,000	8 1,001– 2,500	9 2,501 and over
1	21.7	23.2	23.7	24.0	27.2	29.1	27.7	33.5	†
2	34.8	52.1	36.9	42.7	20.0	41.4	41.9	15.3	†
3	27.0	39.4	44.0	44.6	48.2	51.6	52.3	54.9	45.7
4	23.3	39.4	50.8	50.9	50.9	50.2	55.7	53.3	†
5	36.2	45.5	45.5	49.4	53.9	55.0	52.6	54.8	
6	32.3	39.4	43.1	43.6	44.5	47.6	49.8	†	
7	24.3	31.8	33.8	35.5	34.8	37.8	34.6	43.2	
8	28.8	34.3	34.4	33.6	31.9	30.3	29.6	21.7	†
9	11.8	14.1	17.0	18.2	19.0	18.9	17.0	24.9	28.3
10	15.1	15.9	17.6	23.5	27.6	30.7	25.6	23.1	28.4
11	22.0	23.9	31.7	35.9	36.3	38.2	40.9	39.5	43.2
12	28.3	41.1	46.1	47.9	49.5	51.8	55.0	52.5	†
13	28.9	33.6	38.8	37.5	34.5	41.2	40.3	31.5	†
14	30.5	35.5	38.6	40.0	39.9	43.7	45.1	50.5	49.2
15	31.0	35.8	37.5	35.8	33.7	36.6	35.5	38.4	†
16	25.9	29.3	30.0	31.1	32.6	29.5	34.4	35.3	36.1
17	30.8	35.3	35.1	34.5	36.7	36.3	38.9	43.4	43.3
18	32.8	38.2	36.8	43.0	38.6	36.8	38.5	51.4	53.5
19	40.9	52.6	50.7	49.8	53.0	52.8	51.3	51.3	49.5
20	31.4	36.0	39.4	39.4	40.8	35.7	34.6	†	†
All industry groups	24.4	30.8	34.1	35.3	36.5	38.6	38.5	39.1	45.4

† Indicates that the figure for this cell has been merged with that for the previous cell to avoid disclosure of information relating to one or two establishments.
SOURCE: U.S. *Census of Manufactures*, 1939, vol. I, chap. 4, table 3.

number of increases and decreases in productivity between successive size groups for all three indicators on each basis of classification.

There is little over-all divergence between value of product and value added per wage earner. For the second indicator as for the first a marked difference in the proportion of increases to decreases appears on the two classifications, but if the patterns were classified by the criteria of Subsection II much the same results would

TABLE 4-32

SUMMARY OF RESULTS GIVEN BY THREE PRODUCTIVITY INDICATORS, 20 INDUSTRY GROUPS IN THE UNITED STATES, 1939

	Indicator					
	Value of product per wage earner		Value added per wage earner		Wages as percentage of value added†	
	+	−	+	−	+	−
P classification	142	17	131	28	89	70
W classification	68	79	72	75	47	100

† For this indicator a rise in labor productivity from one size group to the next is indicated by a fall in the value of the indicator, and vice versa.

emerge as in Table 4-27. Wages as a percentage of value added, however, shows a substantially smaller number of increases between successive size groups on both methods of classification than either of the other indicators. There is not space to graph the patterns given by the figures in Tables 4-30 and 4-31, but we may say in summary that their outstanding characteristic is irregularity and lack of any clear pattern for either basis of classification taken singly, and we have as yet no theory for the joint interpretation of the patterns, since the bases of classification are neither wages nor value added. If the data were classified by these variables, then the theory of Subsection II would apply directly to the interpretation of the resultant patterns for wages as a percentage of value added, and it seems probable that smoother patterns would emerge than those given by Tables 4-30 and 4-31.

Our conclusions may be summarized as follows:

1. The paradox of apparently conflicting results on the relationship of labor productivity to size of establishment is a statistical rather than an economic matter, the essential condition for the

emergence of the paradox being the spread of the original W, P scatter in relation to the classification grid adopted for the two variables, value of product and number of wage earners per establishment.

2. Valid inferences about the relationship of labor productivity to size can only be properly established by joint consideration of both patterns in terms of the criteria developed in Subsection II.

3. Perhaps the most emphatic warning against trusting either basis singly is provided by case A above, where a zero correlation between value of product and number of wage earners produces steadily increasing productivity on the one classification, and steadily decreasing productivity on the other.

4. If, however, only a single basis of classification is possible, then it seems preferable to classify by number of wage earners, for the reasons outlined on page 125 above.

5. If the selected indicator of labor productivity is wages as a percentage of value added, then it is desirable to compute this statistic for establishments grouped by wages and value added, when the theory of Subsection II can be applied directly to the interpretation of the results.

Appendix

It is desirable to explore more fully the nature of the condition for contradictory results from the two classifications, and in order to compare our results with those of Steindl we work with log P and log W. The log of product per worker is then given by log $P - \log W$. If we have a series of points with *constant* log product per worker equal to, say, K, then the coordinates of these points satisfy the equation

$$\log W = \log P - K \qquad (A4\text{-}1)$$

Thus these points are represented by a straight line with slope unity on the log W, log P scatter, and the constant value of log product per worker is given by the intercept on the log P axis, which is positive if K is positive. If $K = 0$, the units of measurement are such that $P/W = 1$, and a negative value of K corresponds to $P/W < 1$.

If log P/W is to increase with increases in log P (or log W), we must have a series of points up the log W, log P scatter where the slope of the line joining successive points is always less than unity; the corresponding condition for decreasing labor productivity is a slope greater than unity. Drawing parallels at $45°$ through the three points Q_1, Q_2, Q_3 on Fig. 4-28 gives the successive values of $\log P/W$ as OR_1, OR_2, OR_3.

Assuming approximately linear regressions, we see that the condition for product per wage earner to increase steadily on the P classification and decrease steadily on the W classification is

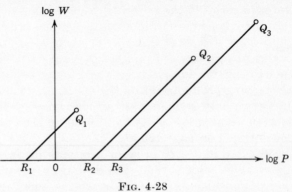

Fig. 4-28

that the regression of $\log W$ on $\log P$ should have a slope of less than unity and the regression of $\log P$ on $\log W$ a slope greater than unity (both slopes referred to the $\log P$ axis). Let

$$x = \log P \qquad \text{and} \qquad y = \log W$$

Then the above condition may be written

$$\frac{E(x - \bar{x})(y - \bar{y})}{E(x - \bar{x})^2} < 1 \qquad \text{and} \qquad \frac{E(x - \bar{x})(y - \bar{y})}{E(y - \bar{y})^2} < 1 \qquad \text{(A4-2)}$$

Define $u = x - y = \log$ value of product per wage earner. It was shown on page 113 above that Steindl's condition was equivalent to $b_{xu} < 1$. Now

$$b_{xu} = \frac{E(x - \bar{x})(u - \bar{u})}{E(u - \bar{u})^2}$$

$$= \frac{E(x - \bar{x})^2 - E(x - \bar{x})(y - \bar{y})}{[E(x - \bar{x})^2 - E(x - \bar{x})(y - \bar{y})] + [E(y - \bar{y})^2 - E(x - \bar{x})(y - \bar{y})]}$$

The inequalities in (A4-2) ensure that the denominator of this last expression is greater than its numerator so that $b_{xu} < 1$, and Steindl's condition is verified. The economic implications of the condition, however, are more easily grasped from the following example, which also illustrates how the labor productivity pattern may be derived for a given distribution in the x,y plane.

Let us retain the x,y,u notation and assume that the x,y density is uniform over the region R, as shown in Fig. 4-29.

This is an idealized picture of the constant productivity case, in which several simplifying assumptions have been made. The

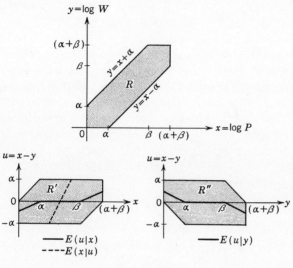

Fig. 4-29

assumption that $f(x,y) = k$ (constant) means that the joint density of W,P is given by

$$f(W,P) = \frac{k}{PW}$$

This is fairly realistic in that it gives a greater density for the smaller values of P and W. The assumption of an identical range, from zero to $(\alpha + \beta)$, for x and y implies an equal range, from unity to $e^{(\alpha+\beta)}$, for W and P, but the assumption of unequal ranges would only affect the top right-hand end of the diagram. Similarly, the way in which we close the top end of the x,y diagram affects the behavior of the labor productivity patterns in the higher size ranges, but our main concern is with the conflicting patterns which emerge in the lower size ranges. The final assumption of continuous variables is strictly inadmissible, but it does not distort the results and materially simplifies the exposition.

From the x,y density we can derive two distributions showing log of value of product per wage earner against log of value of product in the one case and against log of number of wage earners in the other. These are shown in the bottom half of Fig. 4-29. As an example of the derivation of the bounds to the region R' in the u,x diagram, we proceed as follows. For any value of x in the range $0 < x < \alpha$, $y_{\min} = 0$ and $y_{\max} = x + \alpha$. Since $u = x - y$, $u_{\min} = -\alpha$ and $u_{\max} = x$. Similarly for the range $\alpha < x < \beta$, $u_{\min} = -\alpha$ and $u_{\max} = \alpha$, and for the range $\beta < x < (\alpha + \beta)$, $u_{\min} = x - (\alpha + \beta)$ and $u_{\max} = \alpha$.

The distribution of establishments over the x,y plane can thus be transformed into a distribution over the u,x plane and into another distribution over the u,y plane. Under the assumptions made, the u,x and u,y densities will also be uniform over the shaded regions R' and R''. Thus we may write down the regressions $E(u \mid x)$ and $E(u \mid y)$. These are the log labor productivity patterns given by the classification of establishments by log value of product and log number of wage earners, respectively.

For $E(u \mid x)$ we have

$$0 < x < \alpha: \qquad E(u \mid x) = \tfrac{1}{2}(x - \alpha)$$
$$\alpha < x < \beta: \qquad E(u \mid x) = 0$$
$$\beta < x < (\alpha + \beta): \qquad E(u \mid x) = \tfrac{1}{2}(x - \beta)$$

A similar, but reverse, pattern obtains for $E(u \mid y)$ and these two regressions are sketched in the figure. We may notice the similarity of these patterns to those sketched in Fig. 4-22.

The u,x diagram also illustrates Steindl's condition. The regression of x on u is

$$E(x \mid u) = \tfrac{1}{2}[u + (\alpha + \beta)]$$

and this has slope equal to $\tfrac{1}{2}$, which satisfies the Steindl criterion, but the diagram shows the horizontal dispersion about this regression to be so great that little significance can be attached to the actual regression equation.

Finally, we may indicate briefly how the labor productivity patterns for the two classifications may be derived in the general case.[1] Let the establishments have some bivariate distribution

---

[1] We are indebted to L. R. Klein for pointing out that, while the argument of this paragraph is correct in terms of generalized regression functions, it is not necessarily true for regressions calculated in the most conventional way, for example, by a least-squares method.

denoted by $f(W,P)$, where no assumption of continuity is required. From $f(W,P)$ we may derive the two regressions $E(W \mid P)$ and $E(P \mid W)$. The labor productivity pattern given for census data classified by value of product is then

$$\frac{P}{E(W \mid P)} \tag{A4-3}$$

and the labor productivity pattern on the classification by number of wage earners is

$$\frac{E(P \mid W)}{W} \tag{A4-4}$$

It is important to notice that, when we are dealing with P and W in natural units and not in logarithmic form, (A4-3) is *not* equivalent to the regression of P/W on P, for the latter may be written

$$E\left(\frac{P}{W}\,\middle|\,P\right) = P.E\left(\frac{1}{W}\,\middle|\,P\right) \tag{A4-5}$$

and we see that (A4-3) and (A4-5) would only be identical if $E(W \mid P)$ were equal to $1/[E(1/W) \mid P]$; but the former is always greater than the latter, so that the value of product per wage earner given by (A4-3) will always be less than that given by (A4-5) and the shape of the patterns will usually differ also. For the classification by W the two approaches are identical, and (A4-4) is the same as the regression of P/W on W, for the latter may be written

$$E\left(\frac{P}{W}\,\middle|\,W\right) = \frac{1}{W}\,E(P \mid W)$$

5

A Summary of the Empirical Evidence

This chapter summarizes the methods and results of the main empirical studies of cost functions that have been made in the last 20 years. For reasons of both time and space we cannot claim that the summary is completely comprehensive, but an attempt has been made to report on the major results that have been published in the leading professional journals. Attention is centered mainly on *statistical* cost functions, though we have included some studies which involve only the tabulation and averaging of data, without subjecting them to any statistical test. Secondly, we have included only a few examples of the voluminous statistical work that has been done in the field of agricultural production and cost functions. Thirdly, part of the field has already been surveyed, in that a summary account of 44 long-run cost functions has been presented by Wiles.[1] It should be noted that Wiles's summary is confined to long-run cost-output relations, ("costs under total adaptation") and that it includes only nonstatistical cost functions, that is, averages of costs for plants and firms in various size groups with no statistical analysis of the variation displayed or any attempt to allow for the influence of extraneous factors; no *statistical* cross-section cost studies are mentioned in Wiles's review. There is no duplication between the studies reported below and those in Wiles's summary, but we shall quote his final conclusions at the end.

[1] P. J. D. Wiles, *Price, Cost, and Output*, Basil Blackwell & Mott, Ltd., Oxford, 1956, chap. 12, appendixes A and B.

The various studies are summarized seriatim: numbers 1 to 14 deal with short-run cost functions, while the remaining studies are on the long-run function.

1. STATISTICAL DETERMINATION OF COSTS WITH SPECIAL REFERENCE TO MARGINAL COSTS (Joel Dean, *Studies in Business Administration*, vol. 7, no. 1, 1936)

This pioneering study relates to a furniture factory in a small city, manufacturing medium-grade furniture. The firm consisted of a single plant, for which cost data were available at fortnightly intervals. The cost data, however, related to factory cost only, since selling and general administrative expenses were not made available. The period studied was the three years 1932 to 1934; from the 78 two-week accounting periods available Dean selected 47, discarding the other 31 in order to exclude periods in which disturbing factors, unrelated to the cost-output relation, were present. During this 3-year period, capacity and production techniques were unchanged.

The first step in the analysis was the construction of an output index to measure the great variety of models and styles produced. The second step was the correction of the cost data. Factor price index numbers were used for the deflation of cost components; some costs were stablilized at their 3-year average on the grounds that the causes of their fluctuation were not related to output (depreciation, property taxes, fire insurance), while other cost items, which could not be corrected for the serious effects of irrelevant influences, were omitted. Finally an adjustment was made for discrepancies between the time at which costs were recorded and the output to which they relate. The third step was the statistical analysis of the cost relation. Here Dean used graphic multiple correlation techniques to study the effect upon costs of such factors as size of production order, number of new styles, changes in output from the previous period, labor turnover, and quality of product. When the influence of these variables had been taken into account, Dean concluded that the relationship of total cost to output was a linear one.

"The most reliable estimate of marginal cost which can be made from these data is that it is constant at $1.12 per dollar increase in the old warehouse value (output index) regardless of the rate of output." The related conclusion for average cost was that it shows "high values for small output and falls at a diminishing rate as output is increased. However, the curve fails to rise at the maximum of the output range found for the three years studied."

2. THE RELATION OF COST TO OUTPUT FOR A LEATHER BELT SHOP (Joel Dean, National Bureau of Economic Research, Technical Paper no. 2, December, 1941)

This analysis followed the pattern established in Dean's first study. The period studied covered 1935 to 1938, during which time there had been a wide range of output levels but plant, equipment, and technical methods of production had remained unchanged. The findings, based on data from a 4-week accounting period, were

$$_tX_c = -60,178 + 0.770X_2 + 70,181.30X_3 \qquad (5\text{-}1)$$

where $_tX_c$ = total cost

X_2 = output

X_3 = average weight of belting, pounds per square foot

The coefficient of multiple correlation, adjusted for degrees of freedom, was 0.998.

Variance analysis did not reject the linearity hypothesis. As an additional test the incremental cost ratios $\Delta_t X_c / \Delta X_2$ were plotted against output and an approximately horizontal scatter resulted with a mean ratio of 0.767, which is very close to the constant MC of 0.770 in (5-1) above. Dean also fitted a cubic total cost function and the coefficients of the higher terms turned out significantly different from zero at the 2 per cent level on application of the t test. Dean, however, inclined to reject the cubic function because of the very high value of the correlation coefficient in the linear case and also because of the possibility that at high outputs inferior factors of production have to be employed, thus raising marginal costs, and this is not, of course, the reason for the upturn specified in economic theory.

3. STATISTICAL COST FUNCTIONS OF A HOSIERY MILL (Joel Dean, *Studies in Business Administration*, vol. 14, no. 3, 1941)

The mill studied was one of a number of subsidiary plants of a large silk-hosiery manufacturing firm employing highly mechanized equipment and skilled labor. Monthly data were available for 1935 to 1939. The output rate varied from zero to a level approaching the maximum physical capacity of the mill. The size of the physical plant was unaltered, and the quantity and type of equipment remained approximately the same. Technology was stable and management methods essentially unchanged.

Costs were deflated by factor price indices, and a weighted index of individual outputs constructed, the weights being determined on the basis of relative direct labor cost. The statistical results were

$$X_1 = 2,935.59 + 1.998X_2 \quad (R = 0.973) \quad (5\text{-}2)$$

and $X_1 = -13,634.83 + 2.068X_2 + 1,308.039X_3$

$$- 22.280X_3{}^2 \quad (R = 0.988) \quad (5\text{-}3)$$

where X_1 = total costs
X_2 = output
X_3 = time

The incremental cost ratio was uncorrelated with output, with an average value of 1.99.

With respect to average cost, Dean concluded: "Neither the cost observations nor their group averages show any consistent tendency to rise over the extremely high levels of output."

Second- and third-degree total cost functions were also fitted but the coefficients of the higher terms were all less than their standard errors, while the signs of the quadratic term in the parabola and the cubed term in the cubic were both negative, contrary to theoretical expectation. Dean suggested that an important reason for constant MC over the wide output range was the degree of segmentation possible in the plant. There were, for example, 81 identical knitting machines. "Under such circumstances the successive introduction or withdrawal of the machine unit permits wide variability in the services of the machinery despite its overall fixity. Variation in the number of shifts, the length of the working shift and the number of days operated constitutes an additional method of segmentation, and alteration of the speed of machinery may be a third means of segmentation."

4. DEPARTMENT STORE COST FUNCTIONS (Joel Dean, *Studies in Mathematical Economics and Econometrics*, Oskar Lange, ed., Cambridge University Press, London, pp. 222–254, 1942)

Dean selected three departments from a large department store and studied the relationship between costs and sales on the basis of 60 monthly observations covering the period 1931 to 1935. The three departments, coats, hosiery, and shoes, were selected because they displayed fairly large variations in sales volume, not too great heterogeneity of output, and little change in layout, general method of operation, and managerial personnel. The cost relationships found were

$$X_T^C = -35.440 + 1.052X_2 - 0.0019X_2^2 + 0.787X_4$$
$$(R = 0.980) \quad (5\text{-}4)$$

$$X_T^H = -60.764 + 0.347X_2 + 1.557X_4 \qquad (R = 0.957) \quad (5\text{-}5)$$

$$X_T^S = -146.776 + 0.925X_2 + 0.837X_4 \qquad (R = 0.965) \quad (5\text{-}6)$$

where X_T^C = total cost in coat department
X_T^H = total cost in hosiery department
X_T^S = total cost in shoe department
X_2 = number of transactions
X_4 = average value per transaction

The cost elements included in the total cost figure for each department were (1) advertising, (2) salespersons' salaries, (3) other departmental salaries, (4) inside delivery, (5) outside delivery, and (6) direct departmental expense. All allocated general store overhead costs were excluded, in view of the arbitrary nature of the allocation and the fact that interest was centered upon marginal cost.

Dean's findings thus give declining marginal cost with increasing number of transactions in the coat department, and constant marginal costs in each of the other two departments. No relation to cost was found for any of the following variables which were also tried in the analysis:

1. Change in the number of transactions from the corresponding month in the previous year
2. Number of selling days per month
3. Number of selling days per month having unfavorable weather
4. Day to day variability in the volume of transactions

With regard to the fit of his statistical functions, Dean concluded:

> ... The total cost functions are not defined beyond question as being straight lines or parabolas. The unexplained scatter of observations is great enough to permit a cubic of the traditional form to be fitted in each case. However, the curvature would be so slight as to be insignificant from a managerial viewpoint, so that

it could scarcely affect any economic conclusions which might be derived from the linear and parabolic functions. In each instance a higher-order function than that selected was fitted and subjected to critical ratio tests, which indicated that the more complex function did not fit the data significantly better than that chosen.

5. SHORTCOMINGS OF MARGINAL ANALYSIS FOR WAGE-EMPLOYMENT PROBLEMS (R. A. Lester, *American Economic Review*, vol. 36, no. 1, 1946, pp. 63–82)

Lester presents data on variable costs obtained from a small group of firms by questionnaire. Firms were asked the percentage

TABLE 5-1

PERCENTAGE DECLINE IN UNIT VARIABLE COST WITH INCREASE IN SCALE OF OUTPUT

Type of firm	Increase of operations, per cent of plant capacity			
	95–100	90–95	80–90	70–80
Average for 33 firms with maximum profits at 100 per cent capacity	5.5	5.7	7.7	9.5
14 furniture firms	6.4	5.9	4.6	5.2
7 cotton clothing firms	5.6	4.9	6.9	7.5
6 metalworking firms	4.8	7.9	12.5	15.9
6 others	4.7	5.4	9.6	13.9

by which various increases in the rate of plant operation would raise or reduce variable costs per unit of output. Table 5-1 gives a summary of the results.

Constant unit variable costs between 70 and 100 per cent production were reported by 3 firms, while 2 others reported constant unit costs between 90 and 100 per cent production; 3 firms reported rising unit variable costs in the 95 to 100 per cent range at any rate.

This study is open to serious criticism. No information is given on how capacity or variable costs were defined, nor on how entrepreneurs were instructed to treat multiple products, etc. The overwhelming preponderance of replies recording *declining* unit variable cost and the magnitude of the decline at high output levels are surprising, if all variable costs have in fact been included.

Stigler[1] has shown that some of the reported decreases in unit variable costs imply *negative* marginal cost.

6. The Shape of the Average Cost Curve (W. J. Eiteman and G. E. Guthrie, *American Economic Review*, vol. 42, no. 5, 1952, pp. 832–838)

This is another questionnaire study, based on two rather naïve propositions, namely, "Marginal price theory stands or falls depending upon what business men think." . . . "The easiest way to discover what business men think is to ask them."

Thus 1,000 questionnaires containing 8 specimen shapes of average cost curve were dispatched, and 366 replies were received from companies in 32 states. The businessmen were asked to select the curve which applied to their own product(s), and they were instructed to exclude overtime work. The replies were divided almost completely into two groups: 113 companies indicated the *AC* curve which showed a fairly rapid decline followed by a leveling off and then a small upturn at the upper end of the output range, while 203 indicated the *AC* curve which displayed a continual decline throughout the whole output range. One critic,[2] however, was prepared to accept Eiteman's results on the shape of the cost curve but not the inferences which Eiteman proceeded to make about marginal theory.

> His (Eiteman's) results do over-throw the conventional U-shaped cost curves of conventional textbooks and conventional review articles. Amen, and so much the better. But the U-shaped curves are not marginalism, they are merely pretty pictures, just as the hourglass figure is not the human female but the "foundation garment."

7. Note on a Light Plant's Cost Curves (J. A. Nordin, *Econometrica*, vol. 15, no. 3, 1947, pp. 231–235)

Data for 541 eight-hour shifts in a 6-month period were obtained on the two variables Y = total fuel cost and X = output (as percentage of capacity). For each of the two types of coal used, average cost over the 6-month period was computed, and these

[1] G. J. Stigler, "Professor Lester and the Marginalists," *American Economic Review*, vol. 37, no. 1, 1947, pp. 154–157.

[2] M. Bronfenbrenner, "The Shape of the Average Cost Curve: Comment," *American Economic Review*, vol. 43, no. 4, 1953, p. 627.

averages applied to the physical quantities to give a series of corrected cost figures Y. The scatter was distinctly curvilinear and the relationship

$$Y = 16.68 + 0.125X + 0.00439X^2 \qquad (5\text{-}7)$$

was fitted. Variance analysis showed that this was a significant improvement on the linear relation, but that a third-degree function did not improve the fit.

8. ROUND TABLE ON COST FUNCTIONS AND THEIR RELATION TO IMPERFECT COMPETITION: COST BEHAVIOR OF DEPARTMENT STORES (Roswell H. Whitman, *American Economic Review*, Papers and Proceedings, 1939, pp. 400–402)

The relation studied here was the total store variable cost function. No data or statistical relations were presented, but the following conclusion was stated:

> This function has constant marginal costs within the normal range of output, but high marginal costs at the peak. This cost behavior is due to a relatively low efficiency as near capacity output is approached.

9. ROUND TABLE ON COST AND DEMAND FUNCTIONS FOR THE INDIVIDUAL FIRM (*American Economic Review*, Papers and Proceedings vol. 32, supp. 1, March, 1942, pp. 349–350)

This again consisted only of a short summary with no details of the actual investigation.

> Dr. E. Doblin presented results of research conducted by himself and Mr. Seymour Schwarz into the cost functions of Bethlehem Steel and other steel concerns. Costs, defined as total sales value minus net income and adjusted in various ways by the available series of individual cost items, revealed linear functions in all cases and comparatively slight differences in marginal costs as between the concerns studied.

10. STEEL PRICES, VOLUME, AND COSTS (T. O. Yntema, United States Steel Corporation Temporary National Economic Committee Papers, vol. 2, 1940)

This is a study of the United States Steel Corporation based on annual data for 1927 to 1938. Costs were adjusted for factor price changes and a further adjustment to recorded costs was based on the downward trend of costs in relation to volume over the time period involved. The statistical total cost function was

$$X_t = 182,100,000 + 55.73X_2 \qquad (5\text{-}8)$$

where X_t = total cost, dollars

X_2 = weighted output, tons

The components of total cost were (1) interest, (2) pensions, (3) depreciation and depletion, (4) taxes other than social security and Federal income and profit taxes, (5) payroll, (6) social security taxes, and (7) other expenses. The 1927 to 1938 period includes annual rates of operation varying between 17.7 and 90.4 per cent of ingot capacity.

11. THE COST CURVE FOR STEEL PRODUCTION (Kathryn H. Wylie and M. Ezekiel, *Journal of Political Economy*, vol. 48, no. 6, 1940, pp. 777–821)

This is also a study of U.S. Steel but based only on published data, whereas Yntema had unpublished, internal data at his disposal. The authors emphasize the wide range of activities controlled by U.S. Steel.

"Corporation operates, directly or through subsidiaries, ore and coal mines: steamships and railroads: blast furnaces: rolling mills, both hand and continuous strip: tin plate mills: cement plants: steel-fabricating plants for bridges and other heavy structures: and many other productive units." Tonnage of finished steel was used to indicate output because it was the largest item in the sales of the company. In view of the heterogeneity of output and the lack of any attempt on the part of the authors to construct an output index, there seems little point in estimating a cost-output relation. The view of the authors is: "At best the over-all figures for the Corporation can yield only a hazy and approximate picture of the cost function for the operations of individual steel plants."

The authors' first problem was the derivation of cost estimates from published quarterly and annual data. They found that a price index (composite of iron and steel prices) was a fairly good indicator of changes in the price per ton received by the corporation. For quarterly data then they essentially employed the relation

$$\frac{\Pi}{x} = p - \frac{\pi}{x}$$

to estimate average costs per ton Π/x. Π denotes total costs, x the tonnage of finished steel, p the price index, and π net profit before depreciation. For annual data they used the reported revenue of the corporation (excluding intercompany sales). From revenue they subtracted profits available for dividends, bond interest, taxes, and depreciation and depletion charges. The resultant figure divided by the tonnage of finished steel produced was taken as an estimate of direct cost per ton.

For the analyses of both quarterly and annual data, costs were split into the two components of (1) depreciation and depletion and (2) direct production costs, and the relationship of each component to output analyzed. For depreciation the results were

$$X_1 = \$7,850,000 + \$2.08\,Y \qquad \text{quarterly data} \qquad (5\text{-}9)$$

$$X_1 = \$28,750,000 + \$2.25X_2 + f(t) \qquad \text{annual data} \quad (5\text{-}10)$$

where X_1 = total depreciation and depletion charges
$\quad\;\; X_2$ = production of finished steel, tons
$\quad\;\;\; Y$ = quarterly sales, tons
$\quad\; f(t)$ = a time trend in depreciation charges

In the quarterly analysis of direct production costs the three variables found to be related were

$\;\;X_1$ = production costs per ton
$\;\;X_4$ = percentage of capacity operated
$\;\;X_5$ = average hourly earnings, cents (for the whole steel industry)

A seasonal factor was introduced to allow for the fact that the relation between the two factors and cost varied somewhat from quarter to quarter. The use of graphic multiple correlation analysis led to a net relation between level of operation and cost, which showed average production costs declining up to 100 per cent capacity, the curve being steep in the early ranges and much flatter in the high capacity range. In fitting their regression curves, the authors assumed that "the cost per ton might fall with increased output to some point and then rise thereafter. Actually the data showed no indication of a tendency for cost per unit to rise with high output, within the limits of the data available for analysis."

The authors claim that their estimates are quite reliable between 20 and 70 per cent of capacity but are less reliable above 70 per cent. The quarterly figures for percentage of capacity operated range from 101.2 in the second quarter of 1929 to a low of 16.8; there was, however, only 1 figure in the 90 to 100 range and only 3 in the 80 to 90 range.

In the analysis of the annual data, direct cost was found to be related to percentage of capacity operated, average hourly earnings, the price of steel scrap, and the efficiency of labor. Costs per unit again decline throughout the whole range of output. Approximately 85 per cent of the variation in direct costs was accounted for by the independent factors used.

Both the quarterly and annual analyses show direct cost per unit declining throughout the output range. One difference between them is that the quarterly analysis shows constant MC while the annual analysis shows MC declining throughout the output range. This discrepancy is not discussed by the authors.[1]

A final point of difficulty with the study, and presumably with Yntema's also, is that it is not clear whether the cost functions are approximations to short-run or long-run functions. Figures of capacity of U.S. Steel in tons are given in Table C of the Wylie-Ezekiel article.[2] These show a minimum of 17,230,000 tons in the first quarter of 1929, rising steadily to 19,595,000 in the first quarter of 1932, falling to 17,980,000 in the second quarter of 1937 and then rising again. This variation strictly rules out the classification of the functions as short-period; on the other hand, the variation in capacity is too small to justify much confidence in the view that an approximation to the long-run function has been obtained.

12. VARIABILITY OF RAILWAY OPERATING COSTS (E. J. Broster, *Economic Journal*, vol. 48, no. 192, 1938, pp. 674–684)

This analysis was based on annual data for 1928 to 1937 from the Ministry of Transport's Annual Returns of the British Railways.

All recorded costs were included except local rates and law and parliamentary expenses. Costs were corrected for changes in

[1] See, however, a separate article by the same authors, "Cost Function for the Steel Industry," *Journal of the American Statistical Association*, vol. 36, no. 213, 1941, pp. 91–99, in which some of their results are compared with those of Yntema.

[2] Kathryn H. Wylie and M. Ezekiel, "The Cost Curve for Steel Production," *Journal of Political Economy*, vol. 48, no. 6, 1940, pp. 818–819.

salaries, wages, and material prices. After these adjustments a number of graphic experiments were carried out to see whether costs (after allowing for variations in output) were shifting with the passage of time. Broster concluded ". . . operating cost per unit declined with remarkable steadiness in geometric rather than arithmetic progression. The rate of fall approximated closely to 1.17 per cent per annum." Costs were then adjusted for this time trend and correlated with measures of output. Linear relations were fitted, any curvature in the regressions being "graphically imperceptible."

$$E = 0.5475P + 1.6564F + 91{,}170{,}000 \qquad (5\text{-}11)$$

$$E = 0.1000M_p + 0.3680M_f + 54{,}250{,}000 \qquad (5\text{-}12)$$

where E = corrected costs, pounds
P = passenger miles, thousands
F = net ton-miles, thousands
M_p = coaching train miles
M_f = freight train miles

and both equations refer to the level of efficiency and prices ruling in 1937.

13. COMPETITION IN THE RAYON INDUSTRY (Jesse W. Markham, Harvard University Press, Cambridge, Mass., 1952)

This work contains the results of a cost study specially prepared for the author by the members of the industrial engineering and cost accounting staffs of one of the multiplant rayon producers. One curve shows relative unit cost as a function of rate of capacity utilization.

> Since the computation of total unit cost at each per cent of installed capacity operated is based upon constant factor prices but allows for the most economical adjustment of variable factors, the curve approximates the short-run cost curve of economic theory.

The findings on the short-run cost function are as follows:

> Unit costs rise at an increasing rate as output is curtailed and commence to increase immediately with curtailment below 100 per cent of installed capacity. The shape of the curve is attributable for the most part to the high proportion of overhead costs and the relative inflexibility of operations. . . . Although technological advancement has increased the speeds at which spinning machines may be operated, variation from optimum or designed speed in the

short-run is extremely limited and accompanied by production diseconomies. In fact, fairly small increases in machine speeds above designed speed result in a decrease in value product due to the higher percentage of second grade and inferior yarns produced. This accounts for the fact that the short-run cost curve is not extended beyond 100 per cent operating capacity. Producers do not appear to think in terms of producing beyond designed capacity since the cost curve, if extended, would be almost a vertical straight line.

The long-run cost curve had an essentially similar shape, falling fairly sharply at first and then flattening out for the higher plant sizes.

> Unit costs continue to decrease as plant size is increased up to the maximum size plant operated by the firm. . . . The flatness that characterizes the curve between 80 per cent and 100 per cent of the capacity of the largest plant currently operated by the company, indicates that average total unit costs fall very slowly as plant size is increased beyond the present size of its largest plant.

14. ECONOMICS OF BUSINESS ENTERPRISE (W. Rautenstrauch, John Wiley & Sons, Inc., New York, 1939)

This book contains many examples of break-even charts for a variety of corporations in manufacturing and service industries in the United States. The charts shown are historical charts on which recorded annual costs are plotted against the corresponding sales receipts. While distinct shifts in the relationship are observable in most charts, there are long stretches in every chart, which are very well described by a straight-line relation. These linear relations provide some indirect evidence of linear total cost-output relations. Let

z = index of physical inputs of factors
π = index of factor prices
$y = \pi z$ = index of total cost
x = output
p = selling price
$R = xp$ = sales receipts

If inputs depend linearly upon output, we have

$$z = \alpha + \beta x$$

so that

$$y = \alpha\pi + \frac{\beta\pi R}{p}$$

This gives a linear relation between total cost y and sales receipts R provided factor prices and the product price do not vary. If π and p change in the same proportion, the slope of the line will be unchanged, but the intercept will shift.

15. THE LONG-RUN BEHAVIOR OF COSTS IN A CHAIN OF SHOE STORES (Joel Dean and R. Warren James, *Studies in Business Administration*, vol. 12, no. 3, 1942)

Units of a multiple-plant firm were studied in 1937 and 1938.

> Each store individually performs almost all the functions of an independent retail store and might, therefore, be expected to have similar patterns of cost behavior. In addition, such units possess the important advantage of being almost identical with respect to records, merchandise, layout, personnel, and management methods.

A sample of 55 stores was taken, all situated in metropolitan areas and not including any store recently opened or any store selling women's shoes.

The number of pairs of shoes sold was taken as an index of output. From recorded costs the authors omitted the allocations of the general indirect expense and administrative expense, because of the arbitrary nature of the allocation of those central expenses to the individual stores. The main categories included in cost were therefore selling expense (including salaries and wages), handling expense, and building expense.

The pattern of cost behavior was essentially the same in each year and was of the form

$$X_1 = b_1 + b_2 X_2 + b_3 X_2{}^2 \qquad (5\text{-}13)$$

where $X_1 = $ log of total cost

$X_2 = $ log of output

The coefficient b_2 is found to be negative and b_3 positive and significantly different from zero. The elasticity of the total cost function is

$$K = b_2 + 2b_3 X_2$$

$$= -3.128 + 0.916 X_2 \qquad \text{in 1937}$$

$$= -2.460 + 0.760 X_2 \qquad \text{in 1938}$$

Thus the elasticity increases over the whole output range. This gives increasing MC and a U-shaped average cost curve with a minimum where the elasticity of the total cost function is unity, which was at 32,000 pairs of shoes in 1937 and 38,864 pairs in 1938. With respect to this optimum level, the authors remark:

> It is unfortunate that only three stores in the sample have outputs in excess of this critical level of operations, for one can, therefore, have little confidence in the precise magnitude of the optimum rate of operations. This does not mean, however, that the significant change in the elasticity of total cost is attributable only to the influence of the large stores. Even if they are excluded from the analysis, an upward bend occurs in the regression line—in fact, it becomes more marked, and the parabolic shape of the average cost curve is even more clearly defined.

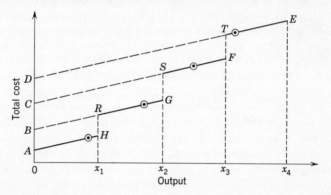

FIG. 5-1. Hypothetical cost function (when additional salesmen must be employed).

The authors attempt to explain this finding of a U-shaped long-run cost function along the following lines. They reject the conventional explanation of diminishing returns to entrepreneurship as not being applicable here, since all the units were controlled by a central organization and the individual store managers had fairly simple and similar tasks to perform irrespective of the size of the store. Nor did the explanation lie with advertising expenses, for these were very small. The largest item in costs was selling expense, and the main item in that was salaries. These were found to have the same relation to output as total costs in (5-13) above. A possible explanation of this may be provided with the help of Fig. 5-1. As sales expand the step function $A\ H\ R\ G\ S\ F\ T\ E$ describes total cost, the steps indicating the hiring of additional salesmen. But this function is probably irreversible downward.

If sales in the largest size store fluctuate temporarily below x_3, total costs will contract along the dotted line DT. The annual observation for any store will be an average of the daily observations. The authors' hypothesis is

> The annual observations tend to lie comparatively closer to the dotted section of the cost curve for large than for small stores. This is because for large stores the observations can range between daily rates of operation of, say, 0 to 50,000, while for small stores the range is only 0 to 5,000. . . . It is apparent from the diagram that a curve fitted to the annual averages shown by the circles will yield a cost function which accords very closely with the empirically determined functions.

This is a plausible hypothesis, but the authors unfortunately have no data on the intensity of utilization or the unevenness in the distribution of sales in stores of varying sizes.

16. PRODUCTION COSTS IN THE GAS INDUSTRY (T. K. Gribbin, *Oxford Economic Papers*, vol. 5, no. 2, new series, 1953, pp. 190–208)

This is a cross-section study of 45 undertakings of the East Midlands Gas Board over the 11-month period from May, 1949, to April, 1950. The undertakings were grouped according to level of output, and the cost figures for each group are presented in Table 5-2.

The net cost into holder in column (3) is the net cost of coal plus production costs plus maintenance of plant and buildings. Increasing size of firm reveals economies in all three components, the economies being particularly marked in production costs, and for the largest size group net cost into holder is less than two-thirds of the figure for the smallest size group. Distribution costs relate to the storage and transmission of gas and include the maintenance of mains and services. Administration consists of the salaries and wages of managers, accountants, and clerks not specifically chargeable to other headings plus the cost of administrative printing, postage, stationery, rent of offices, etc. The allocation of capital charges and headquarters administration costs to each undertaking is *not* included. Administration costs, as defined, show a marked decline with increasing size of undertaking. Total operating costs per therm likewise show a marked decline with increasing size.

TABLE 5-2

OPERATING COSTS

(Pence per therm)

Thousands of therms sold (1)	No. of under- takings (2)	Net cost into holder (3)	Distribution (4)	Collection (5)	Consumer service (6)	Local administra- tion (7)	Welfare (8)	Rates (9)	Total operating cost (10)
101–200	16	12.18	0.74	0.60	0.86	0.80	0.27	0.58	14.31
201–500	8	10.45	1.01	0.64	0.26	0.91	0.38	0.51	13.64
501–1,000	7	8.72	0.45	0.55	0.54	0.73	0.27	0.49	10.67
1,001–3,000	9	9.47	0.61	0.66	0.55	0.53	0.41	0.47	11.59
3,000 and over	5	7.84	0.61	0.67	0.30	0.26	0.48	0.47	10.03

17. THE PURE THEORY OF PRODUCTION APPLIED TO THE FRENCH GAS INDUSTRY (Michael J. J. Verhulst, *Econometrica*, vol. 16, no. 4, 1948, pp. 295–308)

The distinguishing feature of this cross-section study of 25 gas firms in the fourth quarter of 1945 was the use of a conventional profit-maximizing model of entrepreneurial behavior to derive the method of statistical estimation of the parameters of the production function. As one critic[1] has pointed out, the conditions of the French gas industry in late 1945 were not such as to make this assumption of simultaneous profit-maximizing adjustments by gas producers at all reasonable. Verhulst's conclusions, however, were similar to those reached in other studies of the gas industry.

> It seems that the firms of medium size (there are firms of bigger size, but they are not studied in the present paper) are technically more efficient than firms of small size.

18. PRODUCTION RELATIONS IN THE RAILWAY INDUSTRY (G. H. Borts, *Econometrica*, vol. 20, no. 1, 1952, pp. 71–79)

This was a study designed to determine whether increasing returns exist in certain aspects of railway operation.

> The statistical results obtained indicate coefficients of elasticity of variable cost with values of unity or less. If these estimates are accurate, they indicate that increasing or constant returns exist.

Two aspects of railway operation were considered, (1) switching of cargo cars (employment of locomotives in picking up, assembling, and sorting cargo cars into trains) and (2) line-haul operation (transfer of loaded and empty cargo cars between terminals). Because of the status of the railways as common carriers, the quantity of outputs was treated as being beyond the control of the firm. Inputs were divided into unadjustable (roadbed, rolling equipment, and other types of capital equipment) and adjustable (labor, fuel consumption, flow of equipment services, and flow of track and structure services). The statistical procedure was to specify a linear function

$$Y_i = f(Z_1, Z_2, \ldots, Z_n) \qquad (5\text{-}14)$$

[1] Kenneth May, "A Note on the Pure Theory of Production," *Econometrica*, vol. 18, no. 1, 1950, pp. 56–59.

for each adjustable input, the Z's representing outputs and unadjustable inputs. Using data for 76 Class I railways in the United States for 1948, the coefficients of (5-14) were estimated by least-squares methods. From these relations it was possible to derive elasticities of factor use for each adjustable input, the elasticity being the percentage change in factor use accompanying a 1 per cent change in all the output variables, with stocks of equipment held constant. Finally the elasticity of variable cost was found as

TABLE 5-3

COST ELASTICITIES

	Elasticity of variable cost	68% confidence region
Line-haul process:		
Model I	0.9376	±0.0983
Model II	0.5515	±0.1169
Switching process:		
Model I	1.0294	±0.1674
Model II	0.9911	±0.1041

a weighted average of the elasticities of factor use, the weights being the proportion of the total variable cost spent on the particular inputs. The statistical results are given in Table 5-3.

Model II in each case was estimated from variables corrected by division by an index of all physical capital employed. There is, however, no examination of the statistical difficulties caused by a common dividing factor, and the results of Model II should be treated with caution.

The results of Model I do not reject the hypothesis of unit elasticity. No correlation coefficients are given, nor was the assumed linearity of (5-14) subjected to a test or any alternative form of function examined. A final difficulty with the interpretation of these results in terms of constant or increasing returns to scale is the content of variable cost. The flow of equipment services was measured by expenditure on the maintenance of freight equipment, exclusive of depreciation, and similarly the flow of track and structure services was measured by expenditures on maintenance of track and structures for freight service purposes, again exclusive of depreciation. Although certain inputs were considered unadjustable within firms, the use of cross-section data for the study of long-run costs makes it desirable for the full cost of capital equipment to be included, and on these grounds the depreciation figures should have been included.

19. BARRIERS TO NEW COMPETITION (J. S. Bain, Harvard University Press, Cambridge, Mass., 1956)

In a study of 20 manufacturing industries a questionnaire plus interview technique was employed to obtain estimates of (1) the minimum physical production capacity of plant required for

TABLE 5-4

RELATIONSHIP OF RELATIVE UNIT COSTS TO PLANT SCALE IN SEVEN MANUFACTURING INDUSTRIES

	Relative unit costs of production at plant scales corresponding to specified market percentages of either the unsegmented national market or the largest recognized submarket (optimal costs = 100)								
	5	4	3.5	3	2	1.5	1	0.5	0.25
Cement	100		105		115		135		
Rayon		100			108		125		
Soap		100			103		105		
Petroleum refining		100	100.5	101	102	103	105	108	115
Cigarettes	100				101		102		
Tires and tubes					100	101		104.5	105.5
Liquor						100	100.5	101	102

lowest unit costs, and (2) the percentage by which total unit costs would be higher at various smaller plant capacities. For seven of these industries it was possible to estimate the shape of the plant-scale curves, as shown in Table 5-4. No quantitative estimates for the remaining 13 industries could be made on the basis of the questionnaire replies.

A distinctive feature of this study is the sharp distinction drawn between economies of the large *plant* and economies of the large *firm*. A question was included on the economies of the multiplant firm, with the following results:

In 8 industries no definite estimate could be obtained of the extent, if any, of economies of the multiplant firm. This is in spite of the fact that in five of these industries the "Big 4" firms are large enough to encompass from 7 to 25 plants of estimated optimal scale apiece, and that in two others there is a significant degree of multiplant development. In 6 industries (canned fruits and vegetables, petroleum refining, meat packing, fountain pens, copper, typewriters), it was the concensus that economies of the scale of firm beyond the size of a single optimal plant were either negligible or totally absent. . . . In the remaining 6 industries (shoes, cement, steel, gypsum products, soap, cigarettes) perceptible economies were attributed to the multiplant firm.

The cost advantage of the designated multiplant firm over a single plant firm is estimated as slight, small, or at 1 per cent or less in the cigarette, soap, and gypsum product industries. In the steel, cement, and shoe industries it is placed in the range of from 2 to 5 per cent of costs: small but not necessarily negligible.

20. Cost Curves for Electricity Generation (K. S. Lomax, *Economica*, vol. 19, no. 74, new series, 1952, pp. 193–197)

In a cross-section analysis of 37 firms in 1947–1948, regressions of unit cost on capacity and load factor were computed for the northwestern (15 firms) and the southeastern (22 firms) areas of the United Kingdom. Defining

Y = works cost per unit generated, pence
X_1 = capacity of generators, kilowatts
X_2 = load factor

the relationships fitted were

$$Y \propto X_1^{-0.12} X_2^{-0.41} \qquad \text{(Northwest)} \qquad (5\text{-}15)$$

$$Y \propto X_1^{-0.15} X_2^{-0.70} \qquad \text{(Southeast)} \qquad (5\text{-}16)$$

The author concluded "Functions linear in the logarithms are found to be most satisfactory."

Because of the limitations of the data this study only deals with part of long-run costs, namely, the works costs of generation (fuel, salaries and wages of generating station staff, and maintenance and repairs). The cost data employed do not include management expenses, interest charges, depreciation, etc. The findings of declining unit variable cost with increasing size of firm agree with those of Sec. 4-1.[1]

[1] A similar relation is also reported by Joel Dean, *Managerial Economics*, Prentice-Hall Inc., Englewood Cliffs, N.J., 1951, p. 300. A linear relation on a double logarithmic scale gives a good fit to variable costs per kilowatt hour and output for 196 steam generating plants using bituminous coal.

21. THE ANALYSIS OF COSTS OF RETAIL DISTRIBUTION (Arnold Plant and R. F. Fowler, *Economica*, 1939, vol. 6, no. 22, new series, pp. 121–155)

The operating expenses of over 100 large department stores in the United Kingdom were expressed as a percentage of net sales and the results presented for various sizes of store, as shown in Table 5-5.

TABLE 5-5

OPERATING EXPENSES AS PERCENTAGE OF NET SALES,
UNITED KINGDOM DEPARTMENT STORES

	Annual net sales				
	Under £100,000	£100,000– £250,000	£250,000– £500,000	£500,000– £1,000,000	Over £1,000,000
No. of stores	26	29	26	12	13
Administration	5.54	5.07	5.08	4.97	4.88
Occupancy	7.68	6.88	6.15	6.64	5.67
Publicity	2.26	2.64	2.57	4.33	3.01
Merchandising	10.05	9.06	8.88	8.18	7.83
Dispatch	2.12	1.57	2.01	1.86	2.80
Total	27.64	25.21	24.69	25.98	24.20

The authors did not subject the data to any form of statistical analysis or testing, but summarized the averages in Table 5-5 as follows:

> The larger stores show substantial savings in total expenses; and economies are secured mainly in the divisions of Merchandising (very largely in the cost of buying), in Occupancy, and to some extent in Administration. On the other hand it costs them a good deal to reach their larger public as witnessed by their higher costs for Dispatch and Publicity.

An analysis of postwar data for United Kingdom department stores is reported by L. Cohen,[1] in which 162 stores are now analyzed. A new departure was to group the stores into two classes according to whether they were selling high- to medium-priced merchandise or medium- to low-priced merchandise. For each

[1] "Costs of Distribution in Department Stores," *Transactions of the Manchester Statistical Society*, December 12, 1951.

group a similar expense analysis by size of store was carried out as in Table 5-5. Table 5-6 shows the results. The size groups in this table are the same as those given in Table 5-5, no. 1 referring to the smallest size group and no. 5 to the largest. The steady decline of costs with size shown in Table 5-5 is not completely duplicated in Table 5-6. The stores dealing in higher-priced merchandise show lowest costs in the smallest size group and highest costs in the middle size group. Those dealing in the lower-priced

TABLE 5-6

TOTAL OPERATING EXPENSES AS PERCENTAGE OF NET SALES, UNITED KINGDOM DEPARTMENT STORES, 1949

	Size group				
	1	2	3	4	5
High- to medium-priced merchandise	16.30	18.19	19.29	18.70	18.63
Medium- to low-priced merchandise	19.47	17.42	17.85	16.87	17.30

merchandise do display declining costs with size, though the largest size group has slightly higher costs than the second largest size group. Only 2 of the figures in Table 5-6, however, are based on more than 20 observations and no statistical tests have been applied to the data.

22. COST IN RELATION TO SIZE OF FIRM (S. Melman, *Applied Statistics*, vol. 3, no. 1, 1954, pp. 1–11)

This article consists of a very broad survey of administrative and production expense in 1,034 manufacturing firms in the United States in 1937 and 4,107 firms in 1941. The two cost categories distinguished were:

A Selling, general, and administrative expense

P All production expenses, including maintenance and depreciation

Firms were grouped by asset size, so that firms from diverse industries were included in each size group. The two ratios A/NS and P/NS were computed for each size group, where NS indicates net sales. The results for 1937 are given in Table 5-7 and those for 1941 in Table 5-8.

Melman concludes that the decline in the administrative expense ratio is statistically significant, while the slight variation in the production expense ratio is not.

TABLE 5-7

EXPENSE RATIOS FOR 1,034 MANUFACTURING FIRMS, 1937

Asset size, millions of dollars	No. of firms	A/NS, per cent	P/NS, per cent
Under $1	116	17.8	76.7
$ 1–3	255	15.4	76.9
3–5	132	16.2	75.5
5–10	169	13.8	78.7
10–20	129	13.6	78.2
20–50	120	13.3	77.1
50–100	48	14.8	76.8
100–200	34	10.6	78.6
200–500	21	12.8	77.0
Over $500	10	8.6	77.6

Unfortunately such an analysis is too "aggregative" in character to throw any real light on the economies or diseconomies of scale. Net sales may be a useful indicator of size for firms within

TABLE 5-8

EXPENSE RATIOS FOR 4,107 MANUFACTURING FIRMS, 1941

Asset size, millions of dollars	No. of firms	A/NS, per cent	P/NS, per cent
$0.25–$ 1	2,223	14.1	77.0
1 – 5	1,284	12.3	75.9
5 – 10	279	10.9	75.2
Over $10	321	10.0	76.5

a single industry producing a roughly comparable product at much the same price, but when the type of product and its price may vary between firms of different size in the same industry and when unit price can vary widely between different industries the use of net sales to indicate size may be dangerous and misleading. For example, the inclusion of all industries in a single analysis and the computation of ratios for various size groups opens up the type of difficulty discussed in Sec. 4-7. Melman has to some extent met this objection when he reports:

> These (1941) relations of production and administration expense to size also obtain for firms grouped by size classes within industries, though with greater variability among size classes. . . . Similar relationships hold for 17 out of 22 industry groups. In three cases—rubber, furniture, and petroleum and coal—other relationships with size appear for the expense ratios. In the apparel, and printing and publishing industries the general relationships are not determinate owing to the combination of size classes necessary to avoid disclosure of data for individual firms.

Unfortunately, none of these analyses for separate industries has been presented, nor the results of any statistical tests that may have been applied to them. The possibility of price variations with size of firm *within* an industry has not been dealt with. Thus the constancy of production costs to net sales does not necessarily imply that production costs per unit of output remain constant. For example, letting P denote total production costs and x denote output, suppose that average production costs follow the relationship

$$\frac{P}{x} = \frac{a}{x} + b$$

If then selling price declines a little with increase in x, because, say, the large firms charge a lower price because of lower costs or because the smaller firms are turning out a superior, individualistic product, it will be quite possible for P/NS to remain approximately constant.

23. ADMINISTRATIVE COSTS AND SCALE OF OPERATIONS IN THE U.S. ELECTRIC POWER INDUSTRY (James McNulty, *Journal of Industrial Economics*, vol. 5, no. 1, 1956, pp. 30–43)

This study is confined to administrative costs. It is based on data for just under 100 private electric utilities in the United States in 1949, and the analysis is repeated for 1953. Administrative costs consist of all supervision and engineering expenses in production, transmission, distribution, customers' accounting and collecting, and sales promotion.

Total administrative costs were plotted against the value of

plant less depreciation (taken as a measure of the scale of operations) and the following relationships resulted.

$$X_1 = 0.1 + 0.021X_2 \qquad \text{for 1953} \qquad r = 0.951 \quad (5\text{-}17)$$

$$X_1 = -0.1 + 0.024X_2 \qquad \text{for 1949} \qquad (5\text{-}18)$$

where X_1 = total administrative cost
X_2 = value of plant less depreciation

The vertical intercept was not significantly different from zero and
the application of the F test did not reject the linearity hypothesis.
The result, therefore, is constant administrative costs per unit of
output.

24. A NOTE ON THE DERIVATION OF PRODUCTION FUNCTIONS
FROM FARM RECORDS (Gerhard Tintner, *Econometrica*, vol. 12, no.
1, 1944, pp. 26–34)

This study set the pattern for a large amount of work in estimating production functions for various types of agricultural activity.
The results of these studies can shed some light on the nature of
the corresponding long-run cost curve, since they are generally
based on cross-section data on inputs and outputs and it is easy to
make the transition from production function to cost function. A
major deficiency of the studies, however, is the almost continual
use of a single *type* of production function, namely, the Cobb-
Douglas function. This function is often selected on a priori
grounds such as (1) it gives simple estimating procedures, since
the relation is linear in the logarithms of the variables; (2) the
coefficients of the linear relation are estimates of the various partial
elasticities; and (3) the sum of the elasticities indicates diminishing, constant, or increasing returns to scale according as it is less
than, equal to, or greater than unity. This last property is a useful
one from our point of view, though the function type is inflexible
in that it will give one answer out of the three and cannot accom-
modate a transition from, say, increasing to constant to decreasing
returns to scale.

The Tintner study was based on the business records of 609
Iowa farms for 1942. These farms are explicitly stated not to be
representative of the average Iowa farm, for they were probably
under superior management, of larger size and greater profit-
ability than the average farm. Gross profits were adopted, without
any supporting discussion, as a measure of total product, and the

input categories distinguished were land (number of acres), labor (number of months of labor, including hired and family labor and the labor of the operator), farm improvements, liquid assets, working assets, and cash operating expenses. A summary of the main results is given in Table 5-9.

The sum of the factor elasticities indicates diminishing returns to scale for total farming and for all aspects of farming, except

TABLE 5-9

COBB-DOUGLAS FUNCTION: 609 IOWA FARMS, 1942

Type of farming	Number of farms	Adjusted R^2	Sum of factor elasticities
Beef feeders	112	0.727	0.788
Crops	39	0.712	0.770
Dairy	46	0.702	1.130
Hogs	412	0.626	0.900
Total A†	609	0.671	0.866
Total B‡	609	0.671	0.867

† Total A: Working assets included.
‡ Total B: Working assets excluded.

dairy production. However, the hypothesis of constant returns to scale is subjected to a statistical test for all 609 farms and is not rejected. Confidence limits of 90 per cent for the sum of the elasticities are 0.816 and 4.846. The author's two main comments on the results are

> It should be remembered that the important factor, management, has not been included in the analysis. Hence it is entirely possible that there are in reality constant or even increasing returns to scale, if we had been able to include management.

> We want to emphasize again that our results are probably not typical. They describe the conditions of production on the *better* Iowa farms only. We can think of them as representing the upper part of the true production function.

25. PRODUCTION FUNCTIONS DERIVED FROM FARM RECORDS (Gerhard Tintner and O. H. Brownlee, *Journal of Farm Economics*, vol. 26, no. 3, 1944, pp. 566–571)

This is an identical study to the previous one, except that it relates to 468 Iowa farms in 1939. There are, however, some interesting contrasts between the two sets of elasticities, as may be seen by comparing Tables 5-9 and 5-10.

The sum of the elasticities is now generally much closer to unity, although only one category gives a value in excess of unity. Crops shows the highest figure (1.064) in 1939 and the lowest (0.770) in

TABLE 5-10

COBB-DOUGLAS FUNCTION: 468 IOWA FARMS, 1939

Type of farming	Number of farms	Adjusted R^2	Sum of factor elasticities
Hog	234	0.738	0.947
Beef feeder	124	0.659	0.996
Dairy	32	0.747	0.882
Crops	58	0.767	1.064
General	20	0.833	0.962
Total	468	0.739	0.987

1942. Dairy farming does the reverse, showing the highest figure (1.130) in 1942 and the lowest (0.882) in 1939.

26. PRODUCTION FUNCTIONS FOR A RANDOM SAMPLE OF FARMS (Earl O. Heady, *Journal of Farm Economics*, vol. 28, no. 4, 1946, pp. 989–1004)

A main objective of this study was to derive production functions for a more representative group of farms than the rather special groups of the previous two studies reported above. Thus the work was based on a random sample of 738 Iowa farms for 1939. A more acceptable definition of total product was used in that it included cash sales, home consumption, and inventory increases, though a somewhat debatable inclusion is government payments to farmers. Input categories distinguished were real estate, including the value of both land and improvements, labor, machinery and equipment, livestock, and cash operating expense. Separate functions were fitted to various farm groups. The values of R^2 ranged from 0.61 to 0.88, and none of the 13 sums of elasticities exceeded unity, the smallest being 0.7823 and the highest 0.9742. No test of the hypothesis of constant returns to scale was made.

27. Resource Returns and Productivity Coefficients in Selected Farming Areas of Iowa, Montana, and Alabama (Earl O. Heady and Russell Shaw, Iowa State College Agr. Exp. Sta. Res. Bull. 425, April, 1955)

Continued perseverance with the Cobb-Douglas function now yields increasing returns to scale. The F values in Table 5-11 are

TABLE 5-11

Cobb-Douglas Functions for the Four Sample Areas, 1950

Area	Crop function		Livestock function	
	Sum of elasticities	F value	Sum of elasticities	F value
Montana	1.1200	3.85 (8%)	1.0209	0.35
Northern Iowa	1.1527	7.85 (5%)	0.9836	0.21
Southern Iowa	1.2753	7.32 (5%)	1.0986	4.34 (1%)
Alabama	1.1666	6.20 (5%)	0.9765	0.22

those appropriate to testing the hypothesis of constant returns to scale. The crop function in all four areas displays significant increasing returns to scale, but in livestock function only the data for southern Iowa reject the hypothesis of constant returns.

28. Economic Interpretation of Production Function Estimates (Cecil B. Haver, in Earl O. Heady, Glenn L. Johnson, and Lowell S. Hardin, eds., *Resource Productivity, Returns to Scale, and Farm Size*, Iowa State College Press, Ames, Iowa, 1956, pp. 146–150)

The interesting feature of this study is that it gives the results of fitting four separate *types* of production function to the same set of data. The initial study was of 187 farms in the cash-grain area of north-central Iowa in 1947.[1] The variables were

X_1 = output, dollars
X_2 = labor input
X_3 = operating expense
X_4 = current fixed expense inputs

[1] Earl O. Heady, Cecil B. Haver, and Dean McKee, *The Economics of Cash Grain Farming in Iowa*, Iowa Agr. Exp. Sta. Bull. 429, 1955.

Haver obtains the following results for various types of production function:

$$\log X_1 = 0.165 + 0.061 \log X_2 + 0.475 \log X_3 + 0.566 \log X_4$$
$$\text{with } R^2 = 0.72 \quad (5\text{-}19)$$

$$X_1 = 2{,}934 + 0.839 X_2 + 0.644 X_3 + 1.125 X_4$$
$$\text{with } R^2 = 0.71 \quad (5\text{-}20)$$

$$X_1 = 1{,}760 + 1.01 X_2 - 0.000022 X_2{}^2 - 0.098 \times 10^{-8} X_2{}^3$$
$$+ 2.28 X_3 - 0.000012 X_3{}^2 - 0.35 \times 10^{-8} X_3{}^3 + 1.11 X_4$$
$$\text{with } R^2 = 0.71 \quad (5\text{-}21)$$

$$X_1 = -2{,}401 + 1.18 X_2 - 0.000053 X_2{}^2 + 2.66 X_3$$
$$- 0.000085 X_3{}^2 + 1.09 X_4 \qquad \text{with } R^2 = 0.71 \quad (5\text{-}22)$$

It would appear that agricultural economists can "explain" 70 per cent of the variation in production no matter what type of production function they use. The cubic and quadratic terms in (5-21) and (5-22) give no improvement over the linear function in (5-20). This set of data, however, does not enable us to discriminate between a function linear in the actual variables and one linear in the logarithms of the variables. While such functions are qualitatively distinct, they may yield very similar estimates for the cost function, as we have already seen from the results of fitting both types to the electricity data in Sec. 4-1.

29. ECONOMIES OF SCALE: SOME STATISTICAL EVIDENCE (Frederick T. Moore, *The Quarterly Journal of Economics*, vol. 73, no. 2, 1959, pp. 232–245)

This article draws attention to the 0.6 factor rule, developed mainly by engineers. The basic idea underlying this rule is that for many pieces of capital equipment cost varies directly with surface area, while *capacity* is related to volume. If E denotes capital expenditures and C capacity, we may expect a relation of the form

$$E = aC^b$$

So long as b is less than 1, there are economies of scale in the cost of capital equipment. Engineering and cost data suggest an average value of 0.6 for b.

Statistical estimates of b have also been made for a number of *industries* and *products*.[1] The Chilton study was summarized by Moore as follows:

Chilton has estimated values of b for thirty-six products in the chemical and metal industries. In three cases the value was greater than one but in only one of the cases was it so much larger as to be suspect. In the other thirty-three cases the values ranged from 0.48 to 0.91. The average value of b was 0.68 and the median 0.66.

30. THE ECONOMIES OF SCALE (George J. Stigler, *The Journal of Law and Economics*, vol. 1, no. 1, 1958, pp. 54–71)

This article embodies an entirely different method of inferring the nature of the long-run cost curve. The method is termed the survivor principle. The basic postulate is that the more efficient firms will tend to have a higher probability of survival than the less efficient. The following test is then proposed:

Classify the firms in an industry by size, and calculate the share of industry output coming from each class over time. If the share of a given class falls, it is relatively inefficient, and in general is more inefficient the more rapidly the share falls.

Examining the United States data on steel ingot capacity for 1930 and 1951, Stigler concluded:

... There has been a persistent and fairly rapid decline in the share of the industry's capacity in firms with less than half a per cent of the total, so that we may infer that this size of firm is subject to substantial diseconomies of scale. The firms with one-half to two-and-one-half per cent of industry capacity showed a moderate decline, and hence were subject to smaller diseconomies of scale. The one firm with more than one-fourth of industry capacity declined moderately, so it too had diseconomies of scale. The intervening sizes, from two-and-one-half to twenty-five per cent of industry capacity, grew or held their share so they constituted the range of optimum size.

[1] See C. H. Chilton, " 'Six-Tenths Factor' Applies to Complete Plant Cost" in *Data and Methods of Cost Estimation*, a collection of articles from *Chemical Engineering*, 1952; Harvard Economic Research Project, *Capital Coefficients for the Chemical Industry* (hectographed report), May, 1952.

Thus Stigler infers a long-run cost curve for steel ingot production, which is effectively constant over a very wide range of outputs, with a slight upward turn at each end.

The validity of this method depends upon two crucial assumptions, namely, that the firms studied are in effective competition over a single market area, so that none can take refuge behind spatial or product differentiation barriers, and that efficiency in survival is directly correlated with long-run average costs. Even with these two assumptions it is probably realistic to admit that the relative sizes of firms will be influenced by many factors of a random nature, depending upon peculiarities of time, place, persons, and circumstance. If so, one then has an obligation to test any observed changes against what might have come about by chance alone. A χ^2 test applied to the *numbers* of steel ingot firms and plants in the various size groups does not reveal any significant change between 1938 and 1951. No simple test seems appropriate for the figures of percentage of industry capacity accounted for by the various size groups, and they fluctuate in a fashion that makes any inference about the cost curve terribly uncertain, especially in view of the very small number of firms involved. For example, the number of firms with $2\frac{1}{2}$ to 5 per cent of steel ingot capacity increased from 3 to 5 between 1938 and 1951, and accounted for a change from 10.64 to 22.21 per cent of total capacity. The next size group, from 5 to 10 per cent of industry capacity, had 2 firms in 1938 and 1 in 1951; the corresponding percentage of total capacity declined from 11.18 to 8.12. The 10 to 25 per cent of industry capacity size group had just 1 firm in each year, with 13.24 and 16.10 per cent of industry capacity in 1938 and 1951, respectively. Strict adherence to the assumption that survival is linked to costs would give a wavelike cost curve, and the data on *plant* capacity would give an even more pronounced wave; for, if we examine the sign of 1938 capacity minus 1951 capacity for each size group, we get a regular oscillation of positive, negative repeated four times. In view of the small number of units on which the observations are based, Stigler's solution of smoothing the wave is probably the wisest procedure. The survivor principle is the statement of a *tendency*. We would therefore expect the method to work more effectively and unambiguously in an industry where the number of units was sufficiently large to allow a probabilistic tendency to assert itself.

31. PRICE, COST, AND OUTPUT (P. J. D. Wiles, Basil Blackwell & Mott, Ltd., Oxford, 1956)

To summarize 44 sets of data on long-run cost output relationships, Wiles says:

A. C. descends like the left hand branch of a capital U, swiftly at first and then more gently. Decreasing costs with size are almost universal. But the U seldom turns up again. *Sharply increasing costs with size are practically unknown, and even slight increases are rare.* Sixty per cent of the examples obey what we may call the *law of L-shaped costs.* Another 31 per cent show a slight increase of costs in the largest size-class. Most—but by no means all—of these slight increases are well within the expected margin of error that any empirical correlation should show.

SUMMARY

It is not sensible to summarize the statistical studies reported in Chaps. 4 and 5 by further enumeration and classification of the results in various categories since the studies vary greatly in quality, content, and coverage. Two major impressions, however, stand out clearly. The first is that the various short-run studies more often than not indicate constant marginal cost and declining average cost as the pattern that best seems to describe the data that have been analyzed. The second is the preponderance of the L-shaped pattern of long-run average cost that emerges so frequently from the various long-run analyses.

6

A Critique of the Critics

A variety of criticisms has been directed at the methods employed and the conclusions reached in statistical cost studies. The purpose of this chapter is to pass some of these major criticisms in review. It will be seen that there are some which do not stand up to serious scrutiny; others are superficially plausible but can be shown to be incomplete and misleading; and finally there are those whose validity remains more or less intact after scrutiny. The arguments are not taken up in the above order; rather the first six relate to the short-run cost function and the last three to the long-run function.

1. First, it has been suggested that the statistical methods employed impart a bias toward linearity. Ruggles, for example, argues that quite pronounced curvature in MC and AC will give very little curvature in the total cost function.[1] He produces two diagrams of the same over-all size, one showing average and marginal curves and the other the corresponding total cost curve. The former show marked curvature, while the latter is practically linear. Ruggles's concern is with analyses which attempt to establish the nature of the cost-output relation solely by graphical considerations, and for such attempts the criticism is valid. It does not apply, however, to statistical analyses embodying numerical tests of hypotheses. Manipulation of the vertical scale on a diagram cannot then tell us anything about the existence of a linear bias. This can only be established by a consideration of the

[1] R. Ruggles, "The Concept of Linear Total Cost-Output Regression," *American Economic Review*, vol. 31, no. 2, June, 1941, pp. 332–335.

method of statistical inference employed. Actually, if the cost data were as shown by Ruggles, the statistical analysis would yield a cubic total cost function, for he postulates *exact functional* relationships.

The real problem in this context, however, as Ruggles recognizes, is that the cost function, like most economic relations, is stochastic. It is then true that statistical analysis cannot prove that a certain cost relationship is the true one: statistical analysis provides a procedure for the rejection of a hypothesis, if the probability of a particular relationship having generated the sample observations is less than some fairly small preselected value; and several different hypotheses may well be not inconsistent with the observations. Three important points to note, however, are (*a*) that in the majority of cases where statistical tests have been applied, the hypothesis of a linear total cost function has not been rejected, (*b*) that most often no statistically significant improvement on the linear hypothesis is achieved by the inclusion of second- or higher-degree terms in output, and (*c*) that supplementary tests, such as the examination of incremental costs ratios, usually confirm the linear hypothesis.

2. A second source of linearity bias in the statistical analyses is alleged to be the correction of the observed cost data for factor price changes. The theory of cost curves traces out the implications of various hypotheses about the production function on the assumption either that factor prices are constant and independent of the purchases of a firm or that they are dependent upon the firm's purchases. Actual cost observations frequently come from successive time periods during which factor prices may have changed substantially in response to influences other than the firm's purchases. Two common methods of correcting for these factor price changes are deflation of the actual cost figures by a factor price index number or the recalculation of the cost figures by applying some selected set of factor prices to the actual factor inputs of each period.

It has been argued by Caleb A. Smith that, where the proportions in which factors are applied can be varied in response to changes in their relative factor prices, this second method of correction will lead to an overstatement of the costs of every period except the period to which the selected factor prices relate.[1] Smith

[1] Caleb A. Smith, "The Cost-Output Relation for the U.S. Steel Corporation," *Review of Economic Statistics*, vol. 24, no. 4, November, 1942, p. 168.

noted that the ratio of labor to nonlabor factor prices had ranged from 65 to 100 per cent in the years covered by the U.S. Steel study, but he was unable to surmise how the shape of the cost curve might have been affected. In the hands of Staehle, this valid point of Smith's is cited as one reason why one must expect a bias toward linearity in statistical cost functions.[1] It can be shown that Staehle's conclusion has no general validity and that, in fact, in the case postulated by orthodox theory a likely result is an *increase* in the curvilinearity displayed by the cost-output data. A thorough analysis is required, and it seems desirable to examine the problems involved in both types of cost correction.

The analysis has to be carried out for specific types of production function. Suppose that there are two variable factors of production, A and B, the amounts employed in period t being a_t and b_t. Let the production function be

$$x_t = Ka_t^\alpha b_t^\beta \qquad (6\text{-}1)$$

where x_t is output in period t, and K, α, and β are the parameters of the production function. Let $p_t^{(a)}$ and $p_t^{(b)}$ denote the prices of the two factors in period t, and we make the orthodox assumption that, as these factor prices change, the proportion in which A and B are combined is varied to minimize costs for any given output. The familiar marginal productivity condition enables us to express b_t in terms of a_t and the factor prices:

$$b_t = a_t \frac{\beta}{\alpha} \frac{p_t^{(a)}}{p_t^{(b)}}$$

Substituting for b_t in (6-1) gives x_t as a function of a_t, and taking the inverse gives

$$a_t = x_t^{\frac{1}{\alpha+\beta}} K^{-\frac{1}{\alpha+\beta}} \left[\frac{\beta}{\alpha} \frac{p_t^{(a)}}{p_t^{(b)}} \right]^{-\frac{\beta}{\alpha+\beta}}$$

Total cost in period t is, by definition,

$$\Pi_t = a_t p_t^{(a)} + b_t p_t^{(b)}$$

[1] Hans Staehle, "The Measurement of Statistical Cost Functions: An Appraisal of Some Recent Contributions," *Readings in Price Theory*, George Allen & Unwin, Ltd., London, 1953, pp. 273–275.

Substituting successively the expressions obtained for b_t and a_t gives

$$\Pi_t = Cx_t^{\frac{1}{\alpha+\beta}} [p_t^{(a)}]^{\frac{\alpha}{\alpha+\beta}} [p_t^{(b)}]^{\frac{\beta}{\alpha+\beta}} \tag{6-2}$$

where

$$C = K^{\frac{-1}{\alpha+\beta}} \left(\frac{\beta}{\alpha}\right)^{\frac{-\beta}{\alpha+\beta}} \left(1 + \frac{\beta}{\alpha}\right) \tag{6-3}$$

We see from (6-2) that total cost in period t is a function of output x_t, the parameters of the production function, and the prices of the factors in period t. If we assume that factor prices are constant per period, say at levels $p_0^{(a)}$ and $p_0^{(b)}$, then the cost function is

$$\Pi_t = Cx_t^{\frac{1}{\alpha+\beta}} [p_0^{(a)}]^{\frac{\alpha}{\alpha+\beta}} [p_0^{(b)}]^{\frac{\beta}{\alpha+\beta}} \tag{6-4}$$

The price terms in (6-4) may now be merged with the constant C to give a new constant C', and we have the cost function

$$\Pi_t = C'x_t^{\frac{1}{\alpha+\beta}}$$

which corresponds to the production function (6-1). The assumption of a different set of constant factor prices would give the same *form* of total cost function, but with a different constant in place of C'.

If the parameters of the production function are constant from period to period but factor prices vary, then actual costs are given by (6-2). Suppose we are interested in the cost function (6-4). Then it is obvious from a comparison of the two expressions that there does exist, in this case, a price index number whose application to the recorded costs would give the Π_t of (6-4) *exactly*. The required price index number is a weighted geometric mean of price relatives, namely,

$$P_t = \left[\frac{p_t^{(a)}}{p_0^{(a)}}\right]^{\frac{\alpha}{\alpha+\beta}} \left[\frac{p_t^{(b)}}{p_0^{(b)}}\right]^{\frac{\beta}{\alpha+\beta}} \tag{6-5}$$

The application of this result in practice would require knowledge that the production function was of logarithmic form and an estimate of the relative importance of the α, β parameters. Three questions therefore remain for examination:

    a. If an index number of the form (6-5) is used but incorrect weights are attached to the price relatives, what bias will be introduced into the "corrected" cost figures? In particular, will there be any bias toward linearity when $\alpha + \beta \neq 1$?

b. What bias would spring from the second type of cost correction with this form of production function?

c. Do simple forms of index numbers exist which would *exactly* correct observed cost figures for other types of production function?

We shall examine each of these questions in turn. Suppose we use a price index number of the form

$$P_t = \left[\frac{p_t^{(a)}}{p_0^{(a)}}\right]^{w_1} \left[\frac{p_t^{(b)}}{p_0^{(b)}}\right]^{w_2} \tag{6-6}$$

where $w_1 + w_2 = 1$. Corrected costs, $\Pi_t{}'$, are then given by

$$\Pi_t{}' = C x_t^{\frac{1}{\alpha+\beta}} [p_t^{(a)}]^{\frac{\alpha}{\alpha+\beta} - w_1} [p_t^{(b)}]^{\frac{\beta}{\alpha+\beta} - w_2} [p_0^{(a)}]^{w_1} [p_0^{(b)}]^{w_2} \tag{6-7}$$

where C is as given in (6-3) above. The relative bias in the corrected cost figures may then be defined as $(\Pi_t{}' - \Pi_t)/\Pi_t$, where Π_t is given by (6-4). The exponents of $p_t^{(a)}$ and $p_t^{(b)}$ in (6-7) are necessarily equal numerically but opposite in sign. Taking the exponent of $p_t^{(a)}$ as the positive one, we may write

$$\frac{\alpha}{\alpha + \beta} - w_1 = w_2 - \frac{\beta}{\alpha + \beta} = \gamma \qquad \gamma \geq 0 \tag{6-8}$$

Using (6-4), (6-7), and (6-8), the relative bias may be found as

$$\text{Relative bias} = \left[\frac{p_t^{(a)}}{p_0^{(a)}} \frac{p_0^{(b)}}{p_t^{(b)}}\right]^{\gamma} - 1 \tag{6-9}$$

Defining $p_t^{(a)} = c_{1t} p_0^{(a)}$ and $p_t^{(b)} = c_{2t} p_0^{(b)}$, we have

$$\text{Relative bias} = \left(\frac{c_{1t}}{c_{2t}}\right)^{\gamma} - 1 \qquad \begin{array}{l} \gamma \geq 0 \\ c_{1t} > 0 \\ c_{2t} > 0 \end{array} \tag{6-10}$$

Thus the relative bias in period t, for this type of production function, depends upon the *ratio* of the proportionate changes in the factor prices and upon the errors in the weights used in the index number. The extent of this bias for two selected values of γ is shown in Table 6-1.

It is seen that this bias may be positive or negative. It is zero, no matter what the error in weighting the factor price index number, when the two factor prices have changed in the same proportion. For a given error in weighting, the bias increases numerically the further the ratio of the proportionate change in the two factor prices departs from unity. As the error in weighting increases, so does the absolute value of the bias for all c_{1t}/c_{2t} values. When

TABLE 6-1

RELATIVE BIAS
(Per cent)

$\dfrac{c_{1t}}{c_{2t}}$	$\gamma = 0.1$	$\gamma = 0.2$
0.2	−14.9	−27.5
0.5	−6.7	−13.1
1.0	0	0
2.0	7.2	14.9
3.0	11.6	24.6
4.0	14.9	31.9
5.0	17.4	38.0

$\gamma = 0.1$ the relative bias will lie in the range ±7 per cent, provided c_{1t}/c_{2t} lies between 0.5 and 2.0; for the same range of c_{1t}/c_{2t} the bias will be within ±15 per cent when $\gamma = 0.2$. A value of 0.1 for γ implies a fairly large proportionate error in the estimation of the weights. For example, if $\alpha = 0.6$, $\beta = 0.4$, and we take $w_1 = w_2 = 0.5$, then $\gamma = 0.1$, which represents a 17 per cent underestimate of $\alpha/(\alpha + \beta)$ and a 25 per cent overestimate of $\beta/(\alpha + \beta)$.

While the extent of the bias may be fairly great, it is clear that there is no a priori reason why it should produce a tendency toward linearity in statistical cost functions. Where $(\alpha + \beta) < 1$, the true cost function will be convex to the x axis, and a bias toward linearity would require a *negative* correlation between c_{1t}/c_{2t} and x_t. If $(\alpha + \beta) > 1$ a linearity bias would require a *positive* correlation between c_{1t}/c_{2t} and x_t. There is no obvious a priori reason why one or the other correlation should exist, nor why, if the negative correlation exists, it should more likely be associated with the case $(\alpha + \beta) < 1$ than with the opposite case, nor why, if a positive correlation exists, it should more likely be associated with the case $(\alpha + \beta) > 1$. Notice that, if $(\alpha + \beta) = 1$, the true cost function is linear, and the existence of either correlation between c_{1t}/c_{2t} and x_t would give a bias toward *curvilinearity*.

Turning next to the Smith-Staehle problem, we examine for this same production function (6-1) the bias introduced by the recalculation of the cost figures using $p_0^{(a)}$ and $p_0^{(b)}$ as weights to be

TABLE 6-2

RELATIVE BIAS

(Per cent)

$\dfrac{c_{1t}}{c_{2t}}$	$\beta/\alpha = \frac{1}{2}$	$\beta/\alpha = 1$	$\beta/\alpha = 2$
0.25	19.1	25.0	26.0
0.50	5.0	6.0	5.9
0.75	0.9	0.9	0.9
1	0	0	0
2	5.8	6.1	5.0
3	15.5	15.5	12.1
4	26.0	25.0	19.1
5	36.5	34.2	25.4

applied to the actual inputs a_t and b_t. Since the cost minimization condition gives

$$b_t = a_t \frac{\beta}{\alpha} \frac{p_t^{(a)}}{p_t^{(b)}}$$

corrected costs are then

$$\Pi_t' = a_t \left[p_0^{(a)} + \frac{\beta}{\alpha} \frac{p_t^{(a)}}{p_t^{(b)}} p_0^{(b)} \right] \tag{6-11}$$

The true costs in which we are interested are still given by (6-4), and in this case the relative bias is now found to be

$$\frac{\Pi_t' - \Pi_t}{\Pi_t} = \frac{1 + (\beta/\alpha)(c_{1t}/c_{2t})}{1 + (\beta/\alpha)} \left(\frac{c_{2t}}{c_{1t}} \right)^{\frac{\beta}{\alpha+\beta}} - 1 \tag{6-12}$$

Illustrations of this bias are given in Table 6-2. The bias is everywhere positive or zero, as expected. Again, if we consider a range of c_{1t}/c_{2t} between 0.5 and 2.0, the bias is less than 7 per cent. The nonnegative nature of the bias gives a different result from the previous case. Now a positive *or* a negative correlation between c_{1t}/c_{2t} and x_t will lead to an overstatement of the true costs at *both* low and high output levels. Thus if the true cost function is convex from below, as the orthodox theory assumes, the effect of these chance correlations is to *increase* the degree of curvature, while if the true cost function is linear, the effect is to impart a bias toward curvilinearity. Thus Staehle's position is exactly reversed: a bias depends upon the existence of one or other chance correlation, but the bias is one toward *curvilinearity* not linearity. A linear bias could only exist if the observed output levels were confined to a range where the true cost function was concave from below.

Finally, it may be noted that for other simple types of production function no simple form of index number may exist which will transform observed costs exactly into true costs. This is true, for example, of the production function

$$x = 2Hab - Aa^2 - Bb^2$$

where H, A, and B are constants such that $H^2 > AB$. The bias resulting from any particular method of correction may be evaluated above with similar results.

The magnitude of the biases revealed by Tables 6-1 and 6-2 is perhaps surprising. However, they are in general likely to increase the spread of the cost output points in the Π_t direction without imparting any systematic bias toward or away from linearity. They will, unfortunately, augment the stochastical element inherent in costs and thus reduce the discriminating power of a given number of observations below that ideally obtainable, but a systematic bias is dependent upon particular chance correlations between price changes and output levels, and even then the bias may easily be toward curvilinearity rather than the reverse.

It should be emphasized that the whole of this section assumes that the proportions in which the factors are combined are changeable in the short run and are in fact changed in response to variations in relative factor prices. The possible seriousness of the bias has to be carefully assessed in individual cases according to the amount of variation in relative prices in the period under study and the possibilities of factor substitution in the production process.

3. A third source of linear bias in the statistical cost function is alleged to lie in the necessity of working with the time period for which the accounting data have been drawn up. A distinction is drawn between this time period and the unit time period of economic theory, in which the proportions between factors and the rate of output are assumed to be unchanged. It is then suggested

that if the accounting time period consists of several unit time periods, and

if the output is not spread evenly over each unit period, the use of the average rate of output during the [accounting] period assumes a linear cost function and by this assumption biases the statistically determined cost function toward linearity, since the mid-point of a secant connecting any two points on a curve whose second derivative does not change sign lies closer to a straight line connecting the end points of the curve than does the corresponding point of the curve itself.[1]

This point is superficially plausible, but the argument is incomplete and, as we shall see, misleading.

Suppose we make an orthodox assumption that the total cost function in the unit time period of economic theory is

$$\pi_i = \alpha + \beta x_i + \gamma x_i^2 + \epsilon_i \qquad \gamma > 0 \qquad (6\text{-}13)$$

where π_i denotes the total cost associated with an output rate x_i, and ϵ_i denotes the disturbance term. If we had a sample of N pairs of observations on (π_i, x_i), we might compute the least-squares estimate c of γ. A test of the hypothesis $\gamma = 0$ could then be made by computing

$$\text{var } c = \frac{\sigma_\epsilon^2}{N s_{x^2}^2 (1 - r^2)} \qquad (6\text{-}14)$$

and referring the ratio $c/\sqrt{\text{var } c}$ to the normal distribution, where σ_ϵ^2 is the variance of the disturbance term, $s_{x^2}^2$ is the variance of the x^2 values in the sample, and r is the sample correlation coefficient between x and x^2.

Now suppose that the accounting period consists of n unit time periods, and that the accounting data are in the form of total costs Π and total output X. From (6-13), we then have

$$\Pi = \sum_{i=1}^{n} \pi_i = n\alpha + \beta \sum_{i=1}^{n} x_i + \gamma \sum_{i=1}^{n} x_i^2 + \sum_{i=1}^{n} \epsilon_i$$

which may be written

$$\Pi = n\alpha + \beta X + \gamma X^2 - 2\gamma \sum_{i<j} x_i x_j + \sum_{i=1}^{n} \epsilon_i \qquad (6\text{-}15)$$

where

$$X = \sum_{i=1}^{n} x_i$$

[1] Staehle, *op. cit.*, p. 274. See also Smith, *op. cit.*, pp. 169–170.

Since $\sum\limits_{i<j} x_i x_j$ is necessarily positive, it is clear that total costs from the accounting records will be less than the figure that would be obtained by substituting total output X into the function

$$\Pi = n\alpha + \beta X + \gamma X^2 \tag{6-16}$$

obtained from (6-13) by stepping up the fixed cost from α to $n\alpha$ to give the appropriate figure for the accounting period. Consequently, the curvature shown by the accounting data will be *less* than that of the short-run cost function (6-13). In fact, ignoring

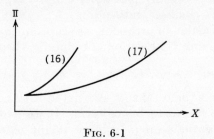

F<small>IG</small>. 6-1

the disturbance term, the limits within which the accounting data must lie are given by (6-16) and

$$\Pi = n\alpha + \beta X + \frac{\gamma}{n} X^2 \tag{6-17}$$

These curves are shown in Fig. 6-1. The relationship (6-16) shows what total costs in the accounting period would be if the whole of the output were produced in a single unit time period, output in each of the other $(n-1)$ unit periods being zero, while (6-17) shows what costs would be if the total output of the accounting period were spread equally over the n unit periods.[1]

It is thus clear that the curvature displayed by the accounting data will be less than that of the ideal, but unobtainable, unit period data. This fact alone is not sufficient to establish a linear bias. The crucial question is the power of accounting data to

---

[1] (6-17) is obtained by maximizing $\sum\limits_{i<j} x_i x_j$ subject to the constraint $\sum\limits_{i=1}^{n} x_i = X$, which gives $x_1 = x_2 = \cdots = x_n = X/n$, and then substituting for $x_i x_j$ in (6-15).

detect this reduced curvature compared with the power of comparable unit period data to detect the curvature of the unit period curve.

To tackle this question, let us assume that

$$2 \sum_{i<j} x_i x_j = \delta X^2 \qquad 0 < \delta < 1 \qquad (6\text{-}18)$$

This implies that the downward pull of the term $2\gamma \sum_{i<j} x_i x_j$ in (6-15) on costs moves proportionately to the square of total output.[1] Using (6-18), we can rewrite (6-15) as

$$\Pi = n\alpha + \beta X + \gamma(1 - \delta)X^2 + \sum_{i=1}^{n} \epsilon_i \qquad (6\text{-}19)$$

From N pairs of observations on Π and X, we might make a least-squares estimate c' of the parameter $\gamma(1 - \delta)$ in (6-19).

To test the hypothesis $\gamma(1 - \delta) = 0$, we would set up a critical region defined by

$$c' > k \times se(c')$$

where k is a constant determined by the level of significance of the test and $se(c')$ is the standard deviation of the sampling distribution of c'. If we work with unit period data, the corresponding critical region for the test of the hypothesis, $\gamma = 0$, is defined by

$$c > k \times se(c)$$

where c is the least-squares estimate of γ in (6-13). The probability of obtaining a sample value of c in its critical region is

$$P_1 = \int_{k \times se(c)}^{\gamma} f(c) \, dc + 0.5 \qquad (6\text{-}20)$$

and the probability of obtaining a sample value of c' in its critical region is

$$P_2 = \int_{k \times se(c')}^{\gamma(1-\delta)} f(c') \, dc' + 0.5 \qquad (6\text{-}21)$$

where $f(c)$ and $f(c')$ denote the sampling distributions of c and c' which, on the assumption of a normal disturbance term, are

---

[1] Provided $n > 2$, this assumption still leaves room for considerable variation in the x_i's for any given values of X and δ.

normal about γ and $\gamma(1 - \delta)$, respectively.[1] The values of P_1 and P_2 depend upon u_1 and u_2 defined as follows:

$$u_1 = \frac{\gamma - [k \times se(c)]}{se(c)} = \frac{\gamma}{se(c)} - k$$

$$u_2 = \frac{\gamma(1 - \delta)}{se(c')} - k \tag{6-22}$$

Since k is constant for any given significance level, the u's depend on t_1 and t_2, defined as

$$t_1 = \frac{\gamma}{se(c)} \qquad t_2 = \frac{\gamma(1 - \delta)}{se(c')} \tag{6-23}$$

From (6-14) above it can be seen that the ratio t_1 is given by

$$t_1 = \frac{\gamma \sqrt{N} s_{x^2} \sqrt{(1 - r^2)}}{\sigma_\epsilon} \tag{6-24}$$

Referring to (6-19), the variance of c' is given by

$$\text{var } c' = \frac{\sigma^2_{\Sigma \epsilon_i}}{N s^2_{X^2}(1 - \rho^2)} \tag{6-25}$$

where ρ denotes the correlation coefficient between X and X^2, and $s^2_{X^2}$ is the variance of the X^2 values in the sample. If we assume the ϵ_i to be independent over time and to have constant variance, then $\sigma^2_{\Sigma \epsilon_i} = n\sigma_\epsilon^2$. Next, in order to compare the power of accounting and unit period observations, we must make some assumption about the spread or dispersion of the output observations in each hypothetical sample. We shall start with the assumption that the coefficient of variation is the same in each case. This would be the case if

$$X = nx \tag{6-26}$$

For example, if the unit period were a month, the accounting

---

[1] P_1 and P_2 have been calculated on the assumption that the critical point for the test lies to the left of the mean of the actual sampling distribution in each case. The conclusion reached below still holds if both points lie to the right of the means. If the inequalities $k \times se(c') < \gamma(1 - \delta)$ and $k \times se(c) > \gamma$ hold, then P_2 is automatically greater than P_1 and our conclusion still holds. The only other possible case is $k \times se(c') > \gamma(1 - \delta)$ and $k \times se(c) < \gamma$, in which case P_1 would exceed P_2. This case, however, requires that $\gamma(1 - \delta)/se(c') < \gamma/se(c)$, which, on the assumptions outlined in the text, is shown to be impossible.

period a year, and we had, say, four annual output observations of 132, 96, 120, 120, then assumption (6-26) means that we wish to contrast the power of these observations with that of the "corresponding" monthly observations 11, 8, 10, 10. Notice that assumption (6-26) does *not* mean that the rate of output must be evenly spread over the n unit periods constituting any given accounting period. For example, the annual output of 132 units could be made up of varying monthly outputs, provided only that they summed to 132 and also satisfied the condition $2 \sum_{i<j} x_i x_j = \delta X^2$.

From (6-26), we then have

$$s_{X^2}^2 = n^4 s_{x^2}^2 \qquad \text{and} \qquad \rho = r$$

Thus the ratio t_2 may be written

$$t_2 = \frac{\gamma(1 - \delta)n^{\frac{3}{2}} \sqrt{N} s_{x^2} \sqrt{1 - r^2}}{\sigma_\epsilon} \tag{6-27}$$

Comparing (6-27) and (6-24), we see that

$$\frac{t_2}{t_1} = n^{\frac{3}{2}}(1 - \delta) \tag{6-28}$$

Thus if the condition

$$n^{\frac{3}{2}}(1 - \delta) > 1 \tag{6-29}$$

holds, the accounting data will have a greater power of detecting curvature, for (6-29) implies $u_2 > u_1$ and hence $P_2 > P_1$. Referring to the definition of δ in (6-18) above, it can be shown that the largest value which δ can assume is $(n - 1)/n$. This occurs when $x_1 = x_2 = \cdots = x_n = X/n$, so that

$$2 \sum_{i<j} x_i x_j = \frac{X^2}{n^2} n(n - 1)$$

Thus the smallest possible value of $(1 - \delta)$ is $1/n$; in this case condition (6-29) becomes

$$\sqrt{n} > 1$$

which is necessarily satisfied by all positive integers greater than unity.

The conclusion therefore is that, on the assumptions made, the power of accounting observations to detect curvilinearity in the cost function is greater than the power of comparable observations on unit periods, even though the effect of the merging of unit periods is to show a curvature less than that of the "true" short-run cost function.

There are two comments to be made on this conclusion. Firstly, it depends upon assumption (6-18), that $2 \sum_{i<j} x_i x_j = \delta X^2$. This assumption implies that, in the absence of stochastic elements, the accounting data would lie on a smooth curve somewhere between the two curves depicted in Fig. 6-1. If this assumption is not exactly fulfilled, then the variance of the disturbance term in (6-19) will be greater than $n\sigma_\epsilon^2$. This will reduce the value of t_2/t_1 below that shown in (6-28). If, for example, the variance of the disturbance in (6-19) were doubled, the value of t_2/t_1 would now be $n^{\frac{3}{2}}(1 - \delta)/\sqrt{2}$. Even if δ takes on its maximum value this t_2/t_1 ratio will still exceed unity for all $n \geq 3$. The second assumption was that the coefficient of variation was the same for the hypothetical samples of accounting and unit period data. This might not be the case. Suppose, to take an extreme assumption, that successive unit outputs x_i were distributed normally and at random about mean value μ with standard deviation σ. The accounting outputs X will then be distributed normally and randomly about mean value $n\mu$ with standard deviation $\sqrt{n}\sigma$. It can be shown that in this case the t_2/t_1 ratio becomes

$$\frac{t_2}{t_1} = \frac{(1 - \delta)\sqrt{n}\sqrt{(2\sigma^4 + n^2\mu^4)}}{2\sigma^4 + \mu^4} \tag{6-30}$$

If μ is at all large in relation to σ this ratio is approximately $n^{\frac{3}{2}}(1 - \delta)$, which is exactly the value obtained in (6-28) above. If, on the other hand, we set the ratio of the two square-root terms at unity, a value which it must in fact exceed, the t_2/t_1 ratio can still exceed unity for appropriate values of δ and n. For example, if $\delta = \frac{1}{2}$, $t_2/t_1 > 1$ provided $n > 4$. Thus even in the case of random outputs it is still quite possible for the accounting data to have greater power of detecting curvature than do the unit data.

4. A fourth objection to the statistical findings of constant marginal cost in the short run is that the observed facts of market behavior contradict these findings:[1]

> . . . If marginal costs were constant over a wide range of output and then rose steeply for each firm, the output of the competitive

[1] G. J. Stigler, *The Theory of Price*, rev. ed., The Macmillan Company, New York, 1952, p. 167.

industry would vary in the short-run chiefly through variations in the number of plants in operation and hardly at all through variations in the rate of output of plants that stay in operation. But this is the opposite of the facts.

The difficulty here is that *these* facts do not provide an unambiguous test of the hypothesis about marginal cost. They do provide a test of a composite, three-part hypothesis, namely, that perfect competition prevails, so that entrepreneurs determine output solely by the principle of securing equality between price and marginal cost, that marginal cost is constant up to high output rates for each firm, and that the level of constant marginal cost varies between firms. Stigler's suggestion is that disagreement between observation and expectation should lead us to reject the second part of the hypothesis.

Suppose, however, that competition is somewhat less than perfect, so that each firm faces a downward-sloping demand function. A depression would cause a general contraction in all these demand functions and even a strict determination of output by equating marginal revenue and constant marginal cost in all firms would tend to give a general reduction in the rate of output of all firms rather than a complete shutdown of higher cost firms. Moreover output determination by the usual marginal revenue—marginal cost calculus—lends an air of spurious precision to a complex and difficult process. Even in the perfect competition model, difficulties arise about the way in which expectations about the future are formed and about the relation of current decisions to these expectations.[1] In general, decisions about output are part of an evolving, dynamic process in which expectations about future sales, price levels, factor supplies, and desired inventory position will all play a part. It does not seem that economists have sufficient empirical confirmation of the simple type of output decision assumed in Stigler's test to use it as a necessary underpinning for a test on the short-run cost function, and, perhaps more seriously, the distinction between perfect and less than perfect competition is crucial for this test.

5. A fifth and major criticism centers around the defects of depreciation figures.[2]

---

[1] See G. B. Richardson, "Equilibrium, Expectations and Information," *The Economic Journal*, vol. 69, 1959, pp. 223–237.

[2] *Cost Behavior and Price Policy*, National Bureau of Economic Research, New York, 1943, p. 76.

Since studies of cost-output relations have relied on financial accounting data which typically utilize straight-line methods of "depreciation," there is introduced into the cost function an important element of linearity which is solely attributable to the accounting techniques. An "economically correct" allocation might yield significantly different results.

The authors of the National Bureau volume seem to favor the method of successive valuation for the determination of the economically correct fixed cost, but they admit that in practice a really correct estimate is impossible.[1] It is, however, clear that for any time period less than the life of the equipment, the accountant's allocable fixed cost will not necessarily coincide with the unknown figure that would be yielded by the method of successive valuation.

This discrepancy only introduces a linear bias into the statistical cost function if use depreciation is in fact nonlinearly related to output. If use depreciation is zero, then the level at which fixed costs are estimated for the period will not affect the statistical estimation of marginal cost either with respect to its shape or position. If a wear-and-tear element enters into depreciation, then the straight-line procedure would understate total costs in periods of high output and overstate them in periods of low output. The error thus introduced depends upon the nature of use depreciation. If, for example, use depreciation is linearly related to output, then the marginal cost estimate from accounting data will be consistently too low, but the accounting data will give an essentially correct picture of the *shape* of the true marginal cost function. If, finally, use depreciation rises sharply at very high output levels, the accounting data based on straight-line depreciation will contain a serious linear bias at the top end of the output scale.

It would seem that no one is yet in a position to generalize about the relative importance of these three hypotheses about use depreciation. A series of cooperative studies by economists and accountants would be extremely helpful. We can, however, in this context disagree with the Institute of Chartered Accountants in England and Wales, who still recommend the straight-line principle,[2] and commend the following suggestion of the American cost accountants:[3]

[1] *Ibid.*, p. 66.

[2] *Recommendations on Accounting Principles*, Institute of Chartered Accountants, London, 1944.

[3] T. Lang (ed.), *Cost Accountants' Handbook*, The Ronald Press Company, New York, 1945, p. 1221.

A compromise between straight line and production methods is obviously called for. This consists of recognizing a fixed minimum charge for depreciation which is present at all levels of activity from zero to 100%. Superimposed on this is a variable charge based on service output or working hours.

6. Criticism has been justly directed against statistical studies of multiple-product firms, where an output index has been constructed to measure changes in the level of a diversified output range. Such an index is usually constructed by weighting quantity relatives with estimates of the average direct costs for each product. As Staehle[1] says,

> This process seems highly objectionable, though it is difficult to see what other solution could be suggested. It indeed amounts to determining output by costs, i.e., to introducing a spurious dependence where measurement of an independent relationship is really wanted.

The fault here is not all the statistician's. In studying the relationship between total costs and an output index, he is trying to force reality into the straitjacket of the single, homogeneous product firm of economic theory, for little progress has as yet been made with the theory of the multiple-product firm. The real world preponderance of multiple-product as against single-product firms is probably the inverse of the space their respective analyses occupy in economic theory. The theorist, in this context, is like a zoologist, whose task is to study the octopus. He reacts to the complexity of the beast by defining an octopus with only a single tentacle and proceeding to study that hypothetical creature very thoroughly, but unfortunately the real octopus with many tentacles may behave very differently from an imaginary octopus with only one.

A possible useful approach to the study of the multiple-product firm is to investigate what cost-output relationships hold for each product separately and to see whether there are any interrelationships between such cost functions. It is also possible to use an output index to provide a test of the linearity and independence of the individual product cost functions. If the weights employed are the estimated average variable costs, then the output index indicates what total variable costs would be if all the individual functions were linear and independent. Correlation with the

---

[1] Staehle, *op. cit.*, p. 270.

actual total variable costs should then give a linear regression with intercept not significantly different from zero and slope not significantly different from unity.[1]

7. A very sweeping criticism of the use of cross-section, contemporaneous accounting data to study the long-run cost function has recently been made by Friedman.[2] He argues that such data "for different firms or plants give little if any information on so-called economies of scale." There are two strands to this argument. First, he considers a competitive industry with no specialized factors of production. The average cost curve would then be the same for all firms and independent of the output of the industry, so that we would expect all cross-section observations to show the same scale of output and the same average cost. Observed differences in the size of firms could only be due to "mistakes" or historical changes in the optimum size of firm. Even then such mistakes should be appropriately valued by a perfect capital market, or written off by internal accounting procedures, so that average cost should still be the same for all firms. When this model is extended to allow for specialized factors of production it is seen that firms may be of different sizes in order to give "appropriate scope" to the specialized resource controlled by the firm, but the capital market and the accountants, when doing their job properly, should still show the same average cost for each firm.

This objection is irrefutable in a perfectly competitive world. We can also in such a world infer the inevitable existence of diseconomies of scale, without dabbling in misleading statistical calculations. The crucial question is what force and relevance does this objection have in a world of less than perfect competition. Consider, for example, electricity generation in the United Kingdom where the size, location, and output of stations are subject to the control of a single authority, or electricity distribution where local monopolies prevail and the size of undertaking is determined largely by the extent of *local* demand. The crucial distinction between perfectly competitive industries on the one hand and "regulated" and imperfectly competitive industries on the other is that, in the former, the size of the market plays no part in determining the size of firm but merely determines the number that can survive, while in the public-utility type of industry the spatial

[1] See Sec. 4-3.

[2] *Business Concentration and Price Policy*, National Bureau of Economic Research, Princeton University Press, Princeton, N. J., 1955, pp. 230–238.

distribution of demand determines both the number *and* relative scale of the firms in the optimal (cost-minimizing) setup. Anything other than a perfectly even spatial distribution of demand involves having firms of various sizes. These size variations are no longer "mistakes," and so there is no reason why accountants should revalue all costs to give identical unit costs in all firms. Similarly, product differentiation and other factors associated with imperfectly competitive markets will make it feasible for firms of various sizes to exist profitably side by side. Imperfect valuation and cost assessments will inevitably exist, but we may expect them to becloud the picture rather than to distort it completely and consistently.

The second strand in Friedman's argument is that costs should be defined as identical with total receipts.[1] In a less than perfectly competitive world, average costs in this sense could then differ between firms, and such differences would reflect not only any possible economies of scale but also variations in the prices charged by large and small firms. The theory of cost curves assumes that in costs we include only those payments necessary to secure the factor services required for the output in question. If costs in this sense are, say, lower in large firms so that higher profits and rents per unit of output accrue in the large firms, it seems both misleading and illogical to redefine costs to include all rents and profits.

Most cross-section studies have not used the Friedman cost concept but have relied on accounting data, which typically include depreciation and maintenance charges but not profits. Ignoring variations in the original cost of capital equipment due to different price levels at the time of purchase, such accounting data provide an index number type of comparison of the total flow of service inputs (both capital and labor) in the various firms. Relating each input figure to the corresponding output thus provides a rough test of the existence of economies of scale.

8. A more general difficulty with the use of cross-section data is the variability of conditions between firms of different size at any given period of time. Variations are possible and likely in the age, type, and cost of equipment. Variations will be present also in the quality of the executives. In fact, even a slight acquaintance with the work of industrial consultants emphasizes the tremendous variations existing in the technical and economic efficiency of

[1] *Ibid.*, p. 234.

different firms. If all firms were on the boundaries of the appropriate production surfaces, as assumed by the economic theorist, the consulting firms would go out of existence through bankruptcy.

These factors make for variations about the cost-scale line. It would be a very unlikely event if the chance correlation of such factors with scale gave the declining cost-scale line found in the large majority of cross-section studies.

One possible difficulty of interpretation of the L-shaped pattern of average costs arises. Is it real evidence of the existence of economies of scale, or does it mean instead that it is the efficient firms which grow big? There are three points to be made here. First, some of the cross-section studies relate to public utilities, such as electricity and gas supply, where the total production required within a defined area is largely dependent on the density of commercial, industrial, and domestic consumers in that area. The existence of local authority or private enterprise monopolies has resulted usually in a single undertaking per area, the size of the plant being geared to the total demand. In such cases the large plants did not emerge from a competitive struggle between a number of small firms, but they nonetheless show substantially lower costs than the smaller undertakings. Such size advantages were the justification for the granting of local monopolies. Secondly, it does not necessarily follow that a small firm with low costs will retain such low costs when it expands. Efficient production on a medium or large scale often requires that the whole plant be designed and constructed *ab initio* for that scale of production. Thirdly, there are many well known and plausible reasons to expect a decline in costs with increasing scale, and while the interpretation of statistical correlations in economics is hazardous, they must in general be viewed in the light of all the other information that one has about the problem in hand. In this case there seems to be impressive agreement between the statistical results and theoretical expectation, with the one qualification that the statistical results do not show with any certainty or regularity the anticipated preponderance of diseconomies with the highest scale levels observed.

9. A final criticism made of cross-section studies is labeled "the regression fallacy." We shall give two examples.

   a. Suppose a firm produces a product the demand for which has a known two-year cycle, so that it plans to produce 100 units in year one, 200 in year two, 100 in year three, etc. Suppose, also, that the best way to do this is by an arrangement that involves identical outlays for hired factors in each year (no "variable" costs). If outlays are regarded as total costs, average cost per unit will obviously be twice as large when output is 100 as when it is 200. If, instead of years one and two, we substitute firms one and two, a cross-section study would show sharply declining average costs. When firms are classified by actual output, essentially this kind of bias arises. The firms with the largest output are unlikely to be producing at an unusually low level: on the average, they are clearly likely to be producing at an unusually high level, and conversely for those which have the lowest output.[1]

b. The second is a much more detailed numerical example due to Stigler.[2]

ASSUMPTIONS

1. There are 41 firms, with normally distributed average outputs (mean output = 100; standard deviation = 40).

2. The output in the given year departs from the average output by a random factor (with mean = 0; standard deviation = average output/2). The random deviations are from W. E. Deming.[3]

3. Hypothesis I. The total cost function of a firm is \$10 times average output.

4. Hypothesis II. The total cost of a firm is \$5 times observed output plus \$5 times average output.

If the random deviation were negative and sufficiently great to make the observed output equal to half the average output for a firm, then hypothesis I would give an average cost of \$20 and hypothesis II an average cost of \$15. The numerical results obtained by Stigler from 41 random deviations are given in Table 6-3. Columns (3) and (4) of this table show a rather typical L-shaped pattern for average costs, although the underlying hypothesis is effectively one of constant returns to scale.

There are two points to be examined in connection with the regression fallacy. The first is whether the fallacy is true in general or only in special cases, and secondly whether it is sufficiently important *quantitatively* to cast serious doubt on the results of cross-section cost studies.

[1] *Ibid.*, pp. 236–237.
[2] We are grateful to Professor Stigler for allowing us to use this example.
[3] *Adjustment of Statistical Data*, John Wiley & Sons, Inc., New York, 1943, p. 252.

Suppose that each firm in an industry has a normal (or average) level of output, to which its capacity is geared. We may then conceive of some distribution of normal outputs for the firms in an industry. Actual output for any firm in a given period may well be greater or less than its normal output due to transient factors of a random nature. Column (5) of Table 6-3 shows that the *average* transient component of output is negative for the firms in the two

TABLE 6-3

NUMERICAL ILLUSTRATION OF THE REGRESSION FALLACY†

Observed output	Number of firms	Average of average cost		Average of the ratios of observed output to average output, per cent
		Hypothesis I	Hypothesis II	
(1)	(2)	(3)	(4)	(5)
Less than 40	8	21.67	15.83	59.6
40–70	9	14.76	12.38	75.7
70–100	6	10.12	10.06	113.0
100–130	5	8.80	9.40	116.0
130–160	4	7.59	8.79	137.0
160–190	3	7.86	8.93	128.3
190–220	3	7.93	8.96	129.3
Over 220	3	6.09	8.05	164.0

† Columns (1) to (4) are adapted from Stigler. In column (5) a figure is added to show the extent of the random variation in output postulated in this example.

smallest size classes and positive for the remaining size classes. This is not just a sampling result due to the particular numbers chosen in Stigler's example, but will be true under fairly general conditions.

Denote normal output by x_1, and let us assume that x_1 has a normal distribution with mean μ and standard deviation σ. Let transient output x_2 also be normally and independently distributed about zero mean with unit standard deviation. Denoting actual output by

$$y = x_1 + x_2$$

we must then study the conditional distribution of x_2, given y, and, in particular, find the mean value of x_2 for any given y. On the assumption of independence between x_1 and x_2, it may be shown that

$$f(x_2 \mid y) = \frac{\sqrt{(\sigma^2 + 1)}}{\sigma\sqrt{2\pi}} \qquad \exp\left[-\frac{1}{2\sigma^2/(\sigma^2 + 1)}\left(x_2 - \frac{y - \mu}{\sigma^2 + 1}\right)^2\right]$$

so that

$$E(x_2 \mid y) = \frac{y - \mu}{\sigma^2 + 1}$$

Thus if the observed output y exceeds the mean output of all firms in the industry μ, the average transient component *for these firms*

TABLE 6-4

x_1	$p(x_1)$	x_2	$p(x_2)$
8	0.2	−1	0.3
9	0.2	0	0.4
10	0.2	1	0.3
11	0.2		
12	0.2		

will be positive; this average, moreover, increases in proportion to the excess of y over μ. Similarly, the average transient component will be negative for any group of firms with an observed

TABLE 6-5

y	$E(x_2 \mid y)$
7	−1
8	−$\frac{1}{2}$
9	0
10	0
11	0
12	$\frac{1}{2}$
13	1

output below the industry average. Although we have assumed independent normal distributions for x_1 and x_2, substantially the same conclusion emerges for any pair of independent, *unimodal* distributions.

A special case where the above conclusion does *not* hold is where x_1 has a rectangular distribution. Suppose, for example, that the distributions of x_1 and x_2 are as given in Table 6-4. Then y will range over the values 7 to 13, and the means of the conditional distributions of x_2 are are shown in Table 6-5. In this case there is no bias over the central range of values, but merely a twist in each tail. This result might have practical importance in the present context if the distribution of firms by normal output was approximately uniform over a substantial output range. However it would appear that conditions favorable to the occurrence of the regression fallacy are probably the general rule.

The quantitative extent of the bias is very difficult to assess, for it depends on the validity and importance of the assumption about transient output. The observed output of a firm in a year (which is the basic time period in most cross-section studies) will depart from the normal output, for which its capacity has been designed, because of (*a*) the general state of the business cycle and (*b*) random factors particular to the firm in question. The general state of the business cycle may be regarded as a transient factor for one year compared with another, but for all the firms in a given industry in a given year it will be approximately a constant factor. Factor (*a*) may in fact be of much greater quantitative significance than (*b*), but it is only (*b*) which is responsible for the distortions of the regression fallacy, and, as the figures in column (5) of Table 6-3 show, very substantial random variations are required to produce a marked distortion of the cost figures.

Taking the ratio of observed to average output for individual firms in Stigler's example, the five lowest figures were 20, 38, 43, 46, and 49 per cent, while the five highest were 159, 165, 168, 184, and 202 per cent. It seems unlikely that random variations of this magnitude could so pervade all reported cross-section studies as to be *solely* responsible for the L-shaped cost curves that appear. The alternative conclusion is that the statistical results confirm the hypothesis of economies of scale, though the *extent* of the economies may have sometimes been exaggerated.[1]

The statistical findings of constant MC in the short run are subject to the criticisms discussed in (6-1) to (6-6) above. The most serious relates to the accounting treatment of the "cost" of capital equipment and the difficulty of ascertaining the user cost of capital assets. MC may rise at extremely high output rates; but over substantial ranges of output, in cases where divisibility or segmentation of capital equipment is possible, it is probably constant.

---

[1] The regression fallacy may be avoided by the incorporation of capacity as a variable in the statistical analysis, as is done at one stage of the study of electricity generation in Sec. 4-1, or by the classification of firms on the basis of the plant size.

As Stigler has emphasized in an important article,[1] the traditional U-shaped *MC* curve rests on the assumption that the capital equipment is indivisible but completely adaptable in form to varying quantities of the cooperating factors. The empirical results suggest that divisible equipment possessing varying degrees of adaptability to cooperating factors is probably more typical of modern industrial processes. The empirical results on long-run costs seem to us to confirm the widespread existence of economies of scale. The evidence on diseconomies is much less certain for, while there is in some studies a suggestion of an upturn at the top end of the size scale, it is usually small in magnitude and well within the range of variation displayed by the data.

The orthodox theory of production with its emphasis on fixed, indivisible factors and variable, divisible, substitutable factors stemmed largely from a rather superficial look at the conditions of agricultural production. The same model with its smooth U-shaped cost curves was easily transferred and elaborated to provide a detailed microeconomic theory of price formation and resource allocation in an industrial society. The fairly hostile reception accorded to the statistical cost studies was accounted for, in part at least, by the apparent conflict between their results and the assumptions underlying the theoretical model. Constant, short-run marginal cost and an L-shaped long-run cost curve were incompatible with any determinate output under perfect competition and indeed with the very existence of the perfect competition of the textbooks. However the conflict is more apparent than real, since most cost studies relate to firms and industries which operate in conditions other than those of perfect competition.

The whole study of business decisions is now being rapidly developed from two different aspects. First, there is the normative work being done in the field of operations research (or management science, or normative microeconomics, to use some alternative titles), and secondly there is an ever-increasing amount of descriptive and econometric work aimed at uncovering first-hand knowledge and testing various hypotheses about the actual decisions of firms on price, output, inventory, fixed investment, etc. A striking feature of both types of work is the emphasis (1) upon uncertainty and the need to form expectations, often quantitative, about future events as a basis for current action and (2) upon the dynamic

[1] G. J. Stigler, "Production and Distribution in the Short Run," *Journal of Political Economy*, vol. 47, no. 3, June, 1939.

evolving character of business decisions, as accumulating experience leads to continuing revisions of plans and expectations. Knowledge of cost-output relations is a vital part of the quantitative information necessary for business decisions, and a field of study that was initially stimulated by a desire to test various economic hypotheses may be expected to play an expanding and useful role in the more detailed and complex work on the firm that is now developing rapidly.[1]

[1] For an outstanding example of an extensive statistical cost analysis developed as an integral part of an analytical study of the American transportation industry, see John R. Meyer et al., *The Economics of Competition in the Transportation Industries*, Harvard University Press, Cambridge, Mass., 1959, especially chaps. 3 to 5 and Appendixes B and C.

Index